Conducting Choirs, Volume 1: The Promising

Conducting Choirs

Volume 1:
The Promising Conductor

A Practical Guide for Beginning Choral Conductors

David P. DeVenney

RogerDean
Publishing Company

A Lorenz Company • www.lorenz.com

Editors: Scott Foss and Kris Kropff
Book Design: Digital Dynamite, Inc.
Music Engraving: Don L. Harris
Cover Design: Jeff Richards

Earlier versions of two chapters here appeared in publications by the American Choral Directors Association. I am grateful for their permission to use them here. Chapter Four: Repertory and Programming appeared as "Repertory and Programming: A Guide for the Young Conductor." 46/6 (December 2005): 77–79. Chapter Five: The Score and the Rehearsal appeared as "Analysis for the Young Conductor." 10/2 (Spring 1997): 4–5.

Roger Dean Publishing Company
A division of The Lorenz Corporation
P.O. Box 802
Dayton, OH 45401-0802
www.lorenz.com

Printed in the United States of America

ISBN: 978-1-4291-1753-1

For Jane

Contents

Visit www.conductingchoirs.com for additional content, free video demonstration clips, and exclusive bonus materials.

Exposition

Successful, musicianly conducting requires the development of a communicative technique. This technique allows an intimate rapport between ensemble and conductor, and its components include hand gestures, eye contact, breath, facial expression, body language, and other factors. Conducting a choir requires the musician to synthesize what one learns in private applied voice study with knowledge gained from the study of music theory, analysis, and music history. This synthesis allows the conductor to understand a score, to form ideas about the music, and to communicate those ideas and emotions to a choir. The choir translates them into sound, with the end goal of making the music and its message accessible and understandable to an audience.

The purpose of this book is to provide a compact but comprehensive guide that helps teach the basics of conducting, rehearsing, and score study. It is not intended to replace the study of conducting with a master teacher, but rather to enhance what is covered in conducting classes and applied lessons. It seeks to provide the student a concise, written source that clarifies the discussion and technical work of class or private study. The chapters here may also serve as a source of further exploration, as they point to more writings on the covered topics in other standard, easily located conducting texts.

Most conducting textbooks are obviously written to be used by students. Too frequently, however, the gestures they define and the approaches they advocate are better suited to advanced students, or to those conducting advanced ensembles. Top-notch ensembles require less basic information than younger, less experienced ensembles. Members of a professional choir like the Los Angeles Master Chorale have years of rigorous training behind them and hundreds of hours of performance experience. They are chosen through competitive auditions and rehearse together for hours; some have sung together for years. Conducting groups like these has its own challenges, of course, but unfortunately, most conductors will not spend their musical lives leading choirs of this caliber. Instead, most choral conductors will lead school choirs, church choirs, or community groups. These less experienced ensembles require different things from their leaders. It is for the conductors and future leaders of these ensembles—the vast majority of choirs in the United States—that I have written this guide.

Conducting pedagogy has always been thorny. First, students are asked to learn a new, holistic way of looking at music and new physical skills to complement that perspective at a relatively late stage in their musical lives. Whereas someone may have studied voice for three or four years prior to college (or piano or other instrument since they were five or six), conducting study usually takes place in the sophomore or junior year. The psychological and interpretive aspects of conducting are vitally important to becoming a good communicator on the podium, but they are difficult to teach either in person or through a text. Like much about conducting, these become self-evident only after gaining real-world experience, something students will not get until they graduate and have conducted their own ensembles for several years. This text may hopefully serve as a welcome review after garnering more experience in front of a choir. Finally, some conducting books continue to separate gestural technique from score study and rehearsal procedures, an arbitrary and artificial position, since communicating with an ensemble is inextricably bound to both performance and rehearsal. In fact, most of the vital work a conductor does occurs in the rehearsal.

In my experience student conductors crave unambiguous answers. One wants me to tell him that if he would only move his arm this way instead of that way, or if she would only make this gesture with the left hand, then the problem will be solved. Would that it were that straightforward! There is no correct way to conduct, as is evident from watching various master conductors. Gesture is personal, like language, and one may only find better ways to communicate effectively, not definitive ways. No stock set of technical answers suffices for all comers.

Too often, conducting is taught as imitation. This rarely leads to effective personal communication. Learning to imitate patterns is not learning how to conduct: slavishly following the gestures of a master teacher will leave the young conductor with only the blandest technical abilities, devoid of meaning since the gesture is divorced from the student's own understanding and personality. Just as singers should sound like themselves and not their voice teachers, so too should conductors look like themselves and not their conducting mentors.

I do not pretend to answer every concern in this text, or to set out inviolable rules for every conductor to follow. But I do aim to help prepare the conducting student to develop the skills and knowledge adequate to leading a choir towards excellent musical performances. Through study, reading, and observation, young conductors will expand their ability to extrapolate musical ideas from a score and to make those ideas understandable to their choir on a higher and more complex level, through effective and meaningful conducting.

Many people have contributed to the writing of this volume, not the least the hundreds of conducting students I have taught. Nothing helps refine ideas like the necessity to explain them many times over to young conductors seeking to understand them. It is to all of these students, both graduate and undergraduate, that I owe a deep thank you. I want particularly to thank Mark Edwards and Jessica Lennick who appear in the photographs in this text. Any number of colleagues, past and present, have also been helpful, sometimes by challenging my ideas but just as often by engaging in fruitful discussion of the issues involved with conducting pedagogy. I have also blatantly stolen ideas from them when the mood suited, as well as from my former teachers, notably Robert Molison, the late Robert Fountain, Earl Rivers, and H. Teri Murai. I both acknowledge my debt to these mentors and proffer my thanks. Thanks also to those colleagues and friends who read drafts of this text, including William Weinert, Robert Molison, Jane Wyss, Craig Johnson, Tony Thornton, Thomas LaFrance, and Robert Barefield. Many thanks to Scott Foss and Kris Kropff for their beautiful work in shepherding this project through to its completion. Finally, my thanks to Kelly Martin and David DeCooman for their continuing support and their interest in this project.

Development

Chapter One

The Right Hand

Introduction

Conducting is communication through gesture. The language of gesture, like all languages, takes time to learn and perfect. Subtlety of speech communication takes years to develop, and so will expressive communication as a conductor. Many elements factor into this unique form of "talking" to a musical ensemble, among them eye contact, body language, and clear mental and intellectual intentions. But the foundation of communicative gesture lies in the bodily movements that we call conducting patterns.

In this chapter, we will discuss basic conducting patterns and their execution. To begin, there are two terms you should know. The first is the *ictus*, or the point of the beat; and the second is the *rebound*, that portion of the beat that lies between two ictus points. An ictus is defined by the rebound, by the change of direction in the pattern at the exact moment of the beat.

Singers live from ictus to ictus—this is where their activity takes place. Their response to your gesture begins on one ictus point and ends on the next. Once the conductor has given the third ictus of a $\frac{4}{4}$ pattern, the singer begins the activity (the notes or rests) that occupies that beat.

The conductor, on the other hand, lives in the rebound of each beat. It is in the rebound of the beat preceding each ictus where the conductor has the sole opportunity to convey performance information: not only tempo (indicated by the speed of the rebound), but also dynamic, style, articulation, and other crucial performance indications.

Traditional conducting styles, at least those outlined in many textbooks, rely on patterns that do not have an ictus point, that moment of rebound that defines the end of one beat and the start of another. The ictus is extremely important in defining a clear pattern and hence in creating concise ensemble singing. The sweeping patterns often illustrated in textbooks, however, do not allow for an ictus point on each beat, rendering them ineffective. If one closely observes experienced, professional conductors in concert, it is rare to see any of them use these sweeping gestures when information needs to be clearly communicated. While experienced ensembles can sing cleanly without continuously provided beats, younger groups usually cannot.

Singers live from ictus to ictus, while conductors live from rebound to rebound.

There is another problem with these sweeping gestures, and that is that they are inherently unbalanced in execution. In a sweeping four pattern, for example, beat one takes X amount of time to execute as one moves, say, ten inches to the conductor's left, to the second beat of the pattern:

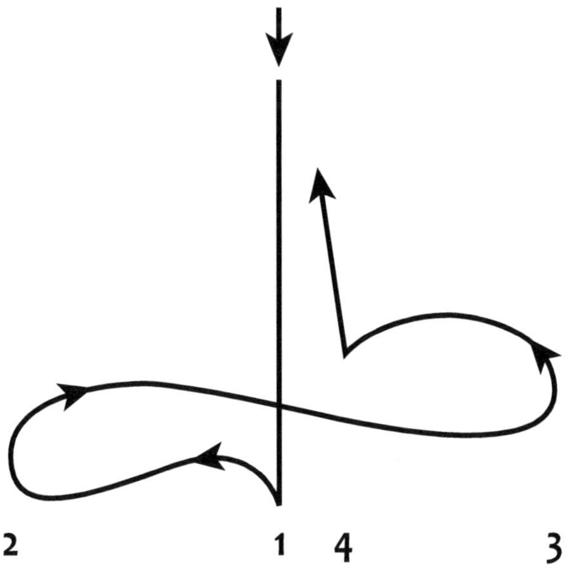

Beat two to beat three covers nearly twice that distance, yet the conductor is expected to cover this greater distance in the same allotted time as he or she covered the distance traveled to the first beat. This means that the conductor must now change the speed of the rebound in order to get to the next beat in the same, exact amount of time.

Changing the speed of the rebound is an inherently dangerous thing to do, since the primary job of the conductor is to convey an accurate tempo in order to allow the ensemble to perform together. To continually change the speed of the rebound invites a distorted tempo. While a good conductor may instinctually rely on his or her innate musicianship to keep a steady pulse, it seems easier to learn from the beginning a technique that allows the young conductor to regulate and maintain this steady pulse.

A modified version of these common sweeping patterns is presented here for two principal reasons. First, the patterns outlined here are more balanced in their design, doing away with the need to constantly make shifts in the speed of the rebound. Secondly, they provide clear ictus points, and consequently relay a strong, steady internalized pulse. Since the primary function of a conductor is to keep an ensemble precisely together, the ability to internalize and communicate a steady pulse is critical to conducting success.

Study and eventual mastery of these exercises and patterns will develop a technical basis for conducting. One learns three-octave scales in every key as a pianist, but that does not imply that the player's upcoming recital will consist of showing off how well she can play scales. Conducting, likewise, does not consist of performing textbook techniques in front of your choir. It consists of drawing on the technical skills you have acquired, combined with experience and musicianship, to develop conducting gestures which are not only individual, but clear, concise, and meaningful. Good communication as a conductor is further reliant upon other factors as well. Among these is meaningful eye contact with your choir, an active and involved posture, good body language, breathing with your singers, and clear musical intentions.

Conducting requires more than reproducing beat patterns in front of your ensemble.

Do you use a baton?

A conducting baton is a magnifying glass. It allows the conductor to make larger gestures more easily. This allows for clear communication to a larger ensemble, which is the reason that instrumental conductors typically use a baton and choral conductors (who often deal with smaller ensembles) more typically do not. Those lines are blurring more frequently in recent times, as more well-known orchestral conductors are opting not to use a baton (freeing their hands to be more expressive), while more choral conductors use one. The choice is really the individual's to make. I usually have my students begin without a baton, but I introduce its use relatively early in the course of study so they can be comfortable using one.

I advocate choosing a light-weight baton anywhere from 12 to 18 inches in length. Use a grip that firmly but lightly grasps the cork or wooden end of the baton. Allow the fingers to curl under; avoid the index finger on top of the baton and don't let the pinkie finger stick out to the side. Hold the baton so the tip is pointed away from you, forming an extension of the arm. Don't allow the baton to turn sideways so that you conduct parallel to the body. Finally, make sure the ictus points are indicated at the tip of the baton, not in the fingers or wrists. Imagine that the tip of the baton is a piece of chalk and that you are writing your pattern on a chalkboard, and you should get the proper idea.

Correct Posture with Baton

Common Pitfalls

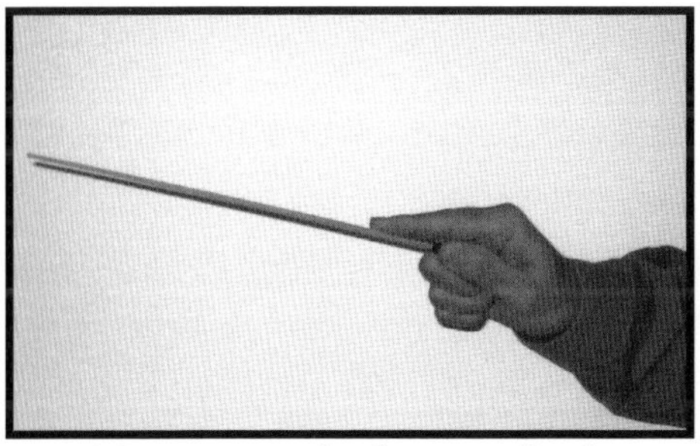

Finger on the baton shaft

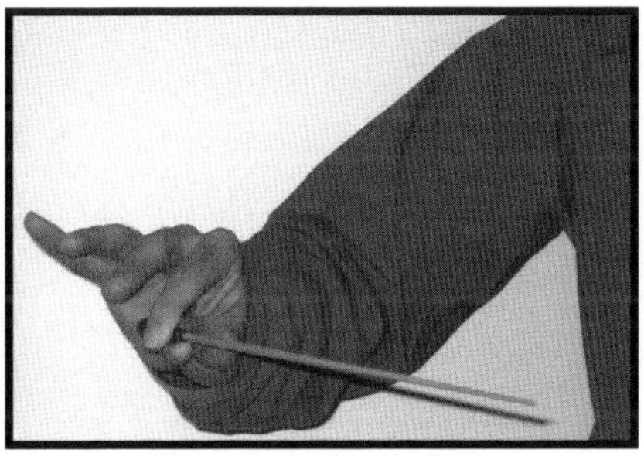

Extended pinkie

Baton turned sideways

Ideally, conductors should be able to conduct clearly with or without this magnifier. If used, remember that the baton should function as an organic extension of the arm and hand that hold it. The key to its effective use is to move the ictus point to the very end of the stick. With practice, the baton can become a familiar and comfortable tool.

Conducting a Pulse

The first step in building these patterns for conducting is to find and hold a steady, recurring pulse. Begin by taking a relaxed body stance, with the shoulders squared and both arms hanging loosely at your sides. Then, slowly lift the right arm from the elbow until the forearm is parallel to the floor. Let your hand be relaxed, with the fingers held lightly together. Try not to move your elbow out from your body, but let it be relaxed at your side (at the same time, do not keep it hugged tightly to your torso).

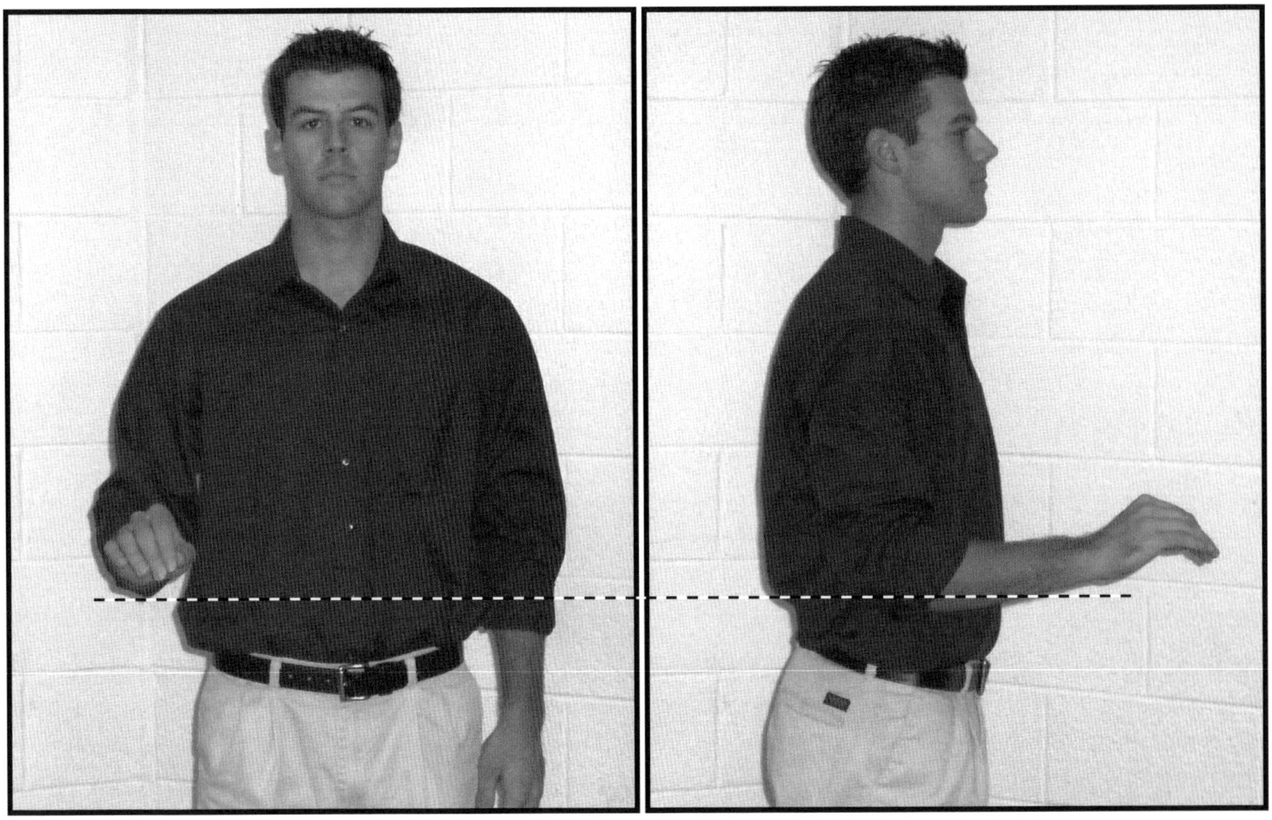

Repeat this several times until your arm begins to feel comfortable in this position. This relaxed position, parallel to the floor, will define the bottom of the *conducting box* and is sometimes called the *conducting plane*. It is at this plane (shown as a dashed line in the figures above) that you will communicate the majority of the information you need to give to your ensemble. By establishing this plane, you are telling your singers or players where the important information will come: here lie the ictus points that provide the consistent pulse that conveys a steady tempo. Note that the conducting box also has a third dimension: depth. Your conducting should also normally lie within a regulated distance away from your torso.

Once you feel comfortable with your plane, raise your hand to chin level, trying not to move your shoulder too much. This level, for now, will constitute the top of the conducting box. When you have established this level, let your arm fall relaxed back to your side. Do this several times, feeling each time the weight of your arm as it falls. This weight is important: begin to internalize the feeling of falling by thinking of it happening simultaneously in the center of the body. Practice letting your arm fall with no muscle tension and no feeling of resistance.

The conducting box occupies an area roughly from the bottom of your chin to your waist and from shoulder to shoulder. The bottom of this box is the conducting plane. The depth of the conducting box should also be consistent.

Next, let your arm fall from the top of the box and stop it at the conducting plane (rather than letting it fall all the way to your side). Don't lose the feeling of the weight of gravity that you had when your arm fell to your side. This feeling of internalized weight is essential to maintaining a steady, even pulse or beat. The bottom of the conducting plane should be slightly elastic so that when your hand falls down, there is a bit of rebound. Don't break your wrist. For now, think of your arm, wrist, and hand as one unit, with the elbow as the primary hinge for movement.

Now pick a fairly relaxed tempo, say quarter note = 80. Simply bounce up and down on the vertical axis you just established, without losing the feeling of weight and rebound at the bottom of the conducting box. Practice this exercise in front of a mirror until the feeling of weight is internalized and the motion looks and feels natural and comfortable. Watch yourself to be sure that your shoulder isn't moving unnecessarily, and that your arm returns to the conducting plane for each ictus point. (The downbeat of the three and four pattern will be performed in the same way as this bounce beat.)

Basic Patterns

There are really only three basic patterns, which suffice for nearly any meter in music: the two, three, and four patterns. The tempo, the meter, and the equality (or inequality) of every beat in a measure are the factors in deciding how to conduct that measure of music.

The downbeat should always drop on an axis from the right shoulder. It should not be placed in the center of the body.

The Three Pattern

We begin with a three pattern, the easiest one to balance and practice. The downbeat of the three pattern is performed like the bounce beat introduced above. For the second beat of the pattern, simply add a smaller bounce to the right of the downbeat. It is smaller for two reasons: it is not as important an ictus to your ensemble as the downbeat, and because the time vs. space ratio needs to stay the same.

The upbeat, or *anacrusis*, is the upward motion of the bounce preceding the rebound just introduced. This can be shown schematically like this:

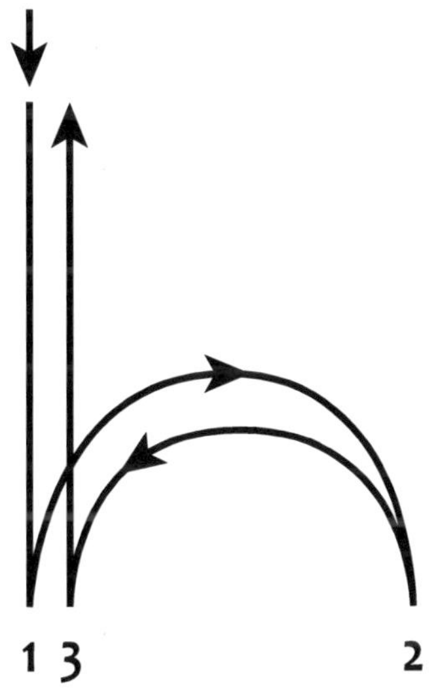

When you practice, make sure that each ictus or beat has rebound to it, and that each maintains the internalized feeling of weight you first practiced. Ensure, as well, that each of the three ictuses lands on a level, consistent conducting plane. The three pattern is also used for measures of $\frac{9}{8}$ meter in a fast tempo.

The Four Pattern

The four pattern is also fairly easy to balance. It is similar to the three pattern, with one extra bounce added to the left side:

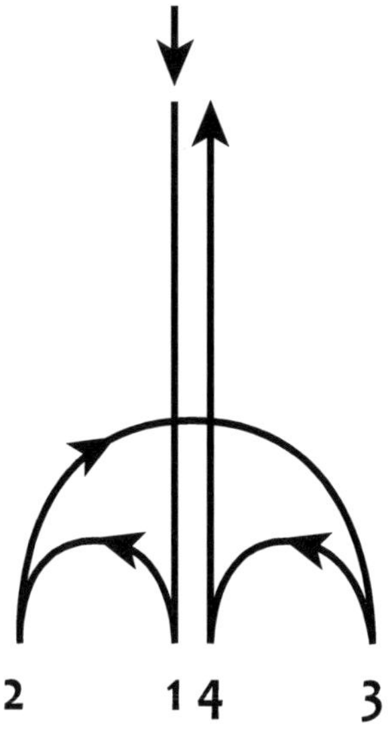

Take care that the distance from ictus two to ictus three is not greater than the distance from the top of the downbeat to the conducting plane, and control the rebounds from beats one, two, and three so that the height of those beats does not overcome the height of the downbeat. As always, make sure that each ictus has a feeling of internalized pulse and weight, and that all ictus points land on an even conducting plane. The first beat should be placed on an axis along the side of your body, not in the center of it.[1] Beat two should not move further left than the center of your body. The four pattern is also used for measures of $\frac{12}{8}$ in a fast tempo.

The Two Pattern

The two pattern is more difficult to do well, so it becomes crucial to concentrate on the size and direction of the rebounds. In the bounce-beat exercise, the downbeat and its rebound were of equal importance. In a two pattern, this is not so, because in music in $\frac{2}{4}$ or $\frac{2}{2}$ meter, the downbeat is the more important beat for your ensemble to identify and it is too easy for both beats to look exactly alike.

Internalize the feeling of weight in each beat. This will help you keep a steady tempo.

For the two pattern, control the rebound after the first beat so that it occupies only about half of the space of the downbeat. It will also be helpful to move the rebound slightly to the right side of the downbeat. The second ictus or beat of the pattern should occupy roughly the same physical space as the downbeat. In the photo at the top of the facing page, the conductor is poised at the end of the rebound for beat 1. (Note: the graphic illustrates what you will draw as the conductor; in the photo, the pattern is reversed because it relates what the musicians will see.) Music in meters of five or six, when the tempo is fast, will also use the two pattern. For meters of five or six when the tempo is slow, other patterns are used.

[1] Centering the axis forces the elbow out and can lead to shoulder tension. Keeping it aligned with the side allows the arm and body to function naturally.

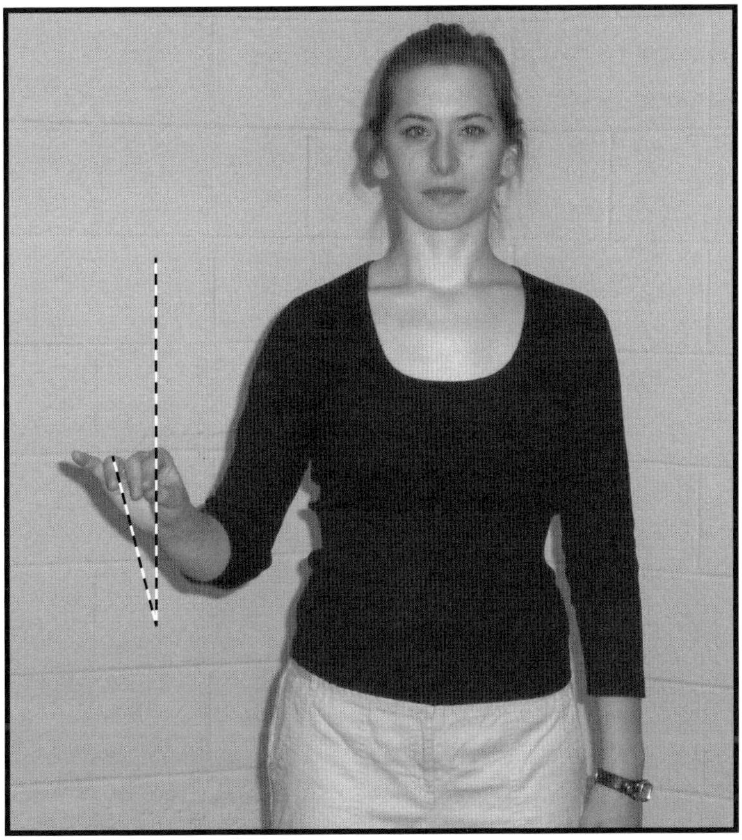

Meters of Five and Six

Music in meters of five or six is grouped into two beats, with each beat further subdivided into groups of two or three. Music written with five beats to the measure is usually arranged in one of two ways: either the music is divided two beats plus three; or it is divided as three beats plus two. If the music is fast enough, you can conduct it in the two pattern, except one beat will be longer than the other, depending on the division of the measure.

In slower tempos, however, you will conduct a pattern that mirrors the division of the meter by placing the correct number of subdivisions on either side of the downbeat. In this case, the cross-motion of the pattern occurs on the primary division of the measure (3+2 or 2+3):

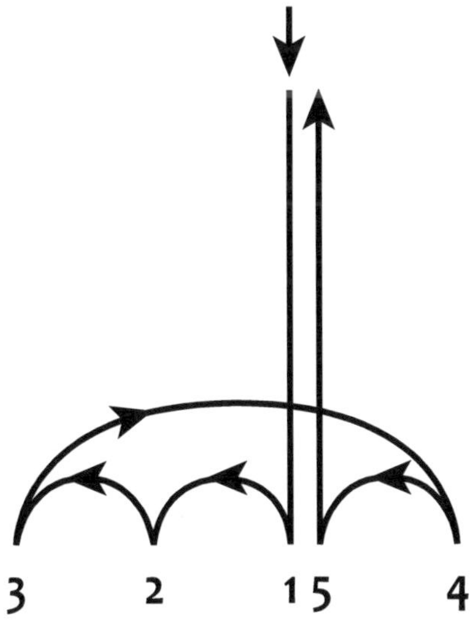

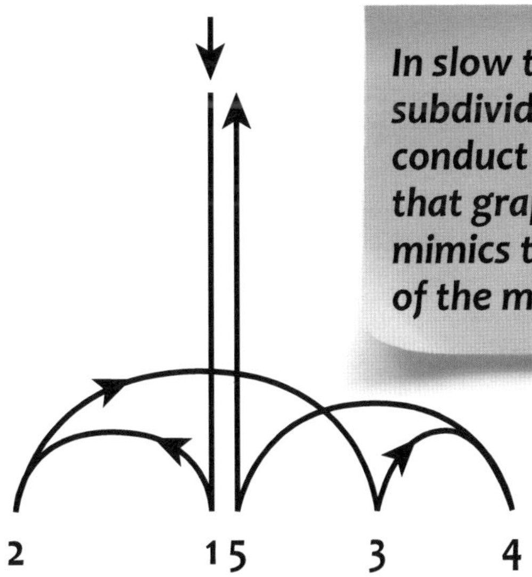

In slow tempos and subdivided meters, conduct a pattern that graphically mimics the division of the measure.

In $\frac{6}{8}$ or $\frac{6}{4}$, when the tempo is slow enough to require the conductor to show all six beats, the following pattern is used:

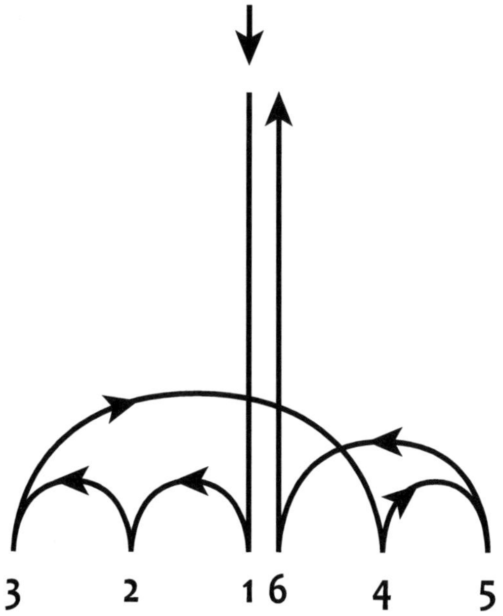

Once again, each of the two beats is given three smaller pulses, one for each subdivision of the beat. The principal division of the meter (into 2 beats) is illustrated by placing the three subdivisions of the beat on each side of the downbeat. Be careful that the rebounds which indicate the subdivisions do not become bigger than the major beats of the measure, and make sure that, big beats or little, each has a feeling of internalized weight and all the ictuses lay on the conducting plane.

Subdividing the Three Pattern

To indicate other meters, we can use the same method of re-articulating ictus points as subdivisions. In each case, one simply adds the correct number of subdivisions on each major pulse. In music that is written in a slow $\frac{3}{2}$ meter, conduct a three pattern and re-articulate the ictus point on each of the three beats, being careful to keep the re-articulation small so the main beats of the measure appear primary.

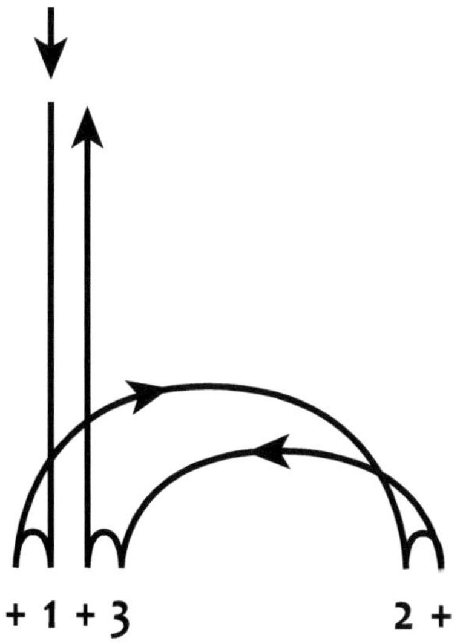

A slow $\frac{9}{8}$ measure would have three beats, each with one full-size ictus and two re-articulations:

When music has seven pulses in a measure, it is commonly divided into three unequal beats: 2+2+3, 2+3+2, or 3+2+2. Each of these is conducted with an unequal three pattern, adjusted according to the principles described previously for conducting meters of five. For 2+2+3, for example, conduct a three pattern, re-articulating the first beat twice (in fact, giving a full-size ictus, followed by a much smaller re-articulation of the ictus), the second beat twice, and the third beat three times (a full-size ictus, and two smaller re-articulations).

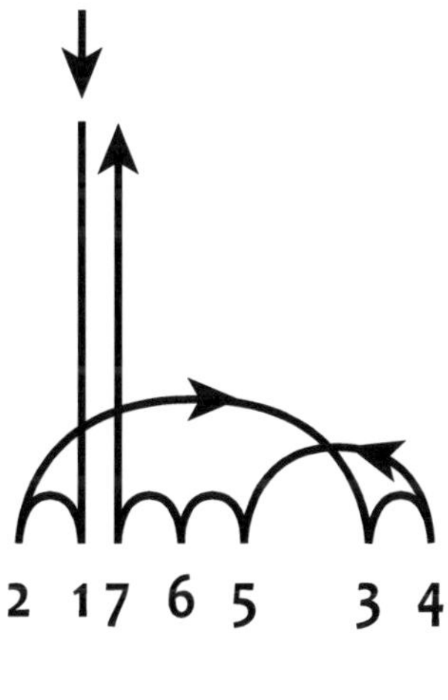

For fast tempos in seven, conduct an uneven three pattern, without re-articulation points, indicating the long beat by delaying the rebound appropriately.

Meters of One Beat

Sometimes, music is written in a meter that requires only one ictus per measure, for example music in a quick tempo in $\frac{3}{4}$ or $\frac{3}{8}$ or, less commonly, music in meters of $\frac{2}{8}$ or where the top number is a 1. For these meters, the solution is simple: use the bounce beat that began this chapter.

Practicing

You must practice all of these patterns until they become second nature. As with any physical skill, you will not be good until you look and feel comfortable and natural doing these patterns. You must be able to conduct any pattern without thinking about it because, as you will learn, a conductor has far too many things to think about and concentrate on, in rehearsal or performance, to stop and think about which direction the arm should move when conducting $\frac{4}{4}$.

Practice all of the patterns introduced in this chapter repeatedly until they feel comfortable and natural. You should always practice in front of a full-length mirror, because doing so will help you see what others will see in you, and you can watch to make sure that your arm and hand are working correctly and that you have no unnecessary tension or movement in your shoulder. Keep the rhythm only in your arm; don't nod your head or tap your foot. Stay relaxed in the chest, shoulders, and neck.

Keep your conducting box consistent: by setting a conducting plane, you have told your ensemble where information will be given to them. The conducting box, for now, should be roughly your upper torso: the top of it aligned with an imaginary line under your chin, the two sides no wider than your shoulders, and the conducting plane approximately waist high and parallel to the floor. The box should have a consistent depth.

A conductor's primary task is to hold a steady tempo, so you must learn to do this without fail. Conductors became widespread in the early Romantic period as groups became larger, and could no longer maintain good ensemble playing over larger distances, and were performing music that was increasingly complex. Where earlier practice put the first violinist or keyboard player in charge, the emerging situation necessitated a person in front of the group to lead. Conducting patterns gradually came into being that naturally indicated the normal stresses of common meters. In $\frac{4}{4}$, for example, the most important beat (the downbeat) gets the most forceful gesture; the second most important beat (commonly the third beat) is illustrated by a strong cross gesture; and the two weaker beats get relatively weaker gestures.

Practice holding a tempo by practicing with a metronome. You can learn to memorize tempos by frequently setting one and then checking yourself against a metronome. Conductors are frequently called upon to set numerous tempos during a concert. One can become quite proficient at this through the body's kinetic memory; but it requires patience and practice over a period of time. Internalize the feeling of weight in each beat. This is the primary safeguard you can use to maintain a steady pulse for your ensemble.

Building Skills

Repetitive practicing is what enables your body to develop its kinetic memory. The additional exercises that follow will help you continue to master the physical skills your right arm/hand need for successful conducting.

Begin these exercises at a moderate tempo, conducting with your right arm only. From the start, begin each example by breathing where your singers will breathe when they have to start—that is, a full beat before singing begins (this topic will be explored more completely in Chapter Two).

To start, choose one of the sequences below and perform three measures of each meter given. When finished, loop to the beginning of the sequence and repeat it several times until you can perform it flawlessly, and your arm finds the correct pattern without having to think about it.

When you have mastered performing three measures of each meter, then perform only two. When you have mastered that, perform each meter only once before moving to the next one. Finally, construct other sequences of your own—mixing meters—if you need further drill with these patterns.

Sequences

1. $\frac{2}{4}$ $\frac{3}{4}$ $\frac{4}{4}$ $\frac{3}{4}$
2. $\frac{2}{4}$ $\frac{4}{4}$ $\frac{6}{4}$ $\frac{3}{4}$
3. $\frac{4}{4}$ $\frac{3}{4}$ $\frac{4}{2}$ $\frac{3}{4}$ $\frac{6}{4}$ (quarter note remains constant)
4. $\frac{3}{8}$ $\frac{4}{4}$ $\frac{5}{8}$ $\frac{2}{4}$ $\frac{6}{8}$ (eighth note remains constant)

Further Practice

Examples for practicing each of the patterns introduced in this chapter follow on the next few pages. The examples for each pattern get progressively more difficult, and here is a suggested process for approaching these exercises:

1. The first time through, conduct and silently watch the music as it goes by, hearing it internally. Begin with a slow or moderate tempo. Practice these with the right hand only.
2. The second time, still at a slow tempo, conduct the meter (right hand only) and say "tah" on the rhythms. By doing this, you are engaging both halves of your brain—your conducting arm is controlled by the right brain, while your left brain is engaged in counting.
3. Repeat each example several times without stopping.
4. When you feel comfortable at a slow tempo, go a little faster. Pay careful attention to your pattern always, taking great care that the rebound is steady, the conducting plane is level, and the conducting box is balanced on your body.
5. When you have mastered one example, move on to the next. When comfortable with them all, perform all the examples of a given pattern in a row at a relatively quick tempo. For the example in $\frac{6}{8}$, practice it more quickly by retaining the subdivided pattern and also by conducting it in a two pattern.

Examples for Practicing the Two Pattern

Examples for Practicing the Three Pattern

Examples for Practicing the Four Pattern

Examples for Practicing the Five Pattern

Example for Practicing the Six Pattern

Examples for Practicing Music in Mixed Meters

Use any of the following three short folksongs to gain your first real conducting experience. For now, begin conducting and ask your classmates to enter on the appropriate beat of your first measure. (Starting and stopping the choir are topics covered in Chapter Two.) In using these examples, don't simply follow the words: watch the music as it goes by, anticipating where the choir will breathe and phrase. Breathe with them in those places. Begin to empathize with your ensemble as they sing, and you will have made your first steps towards leading a choir!

Clementine

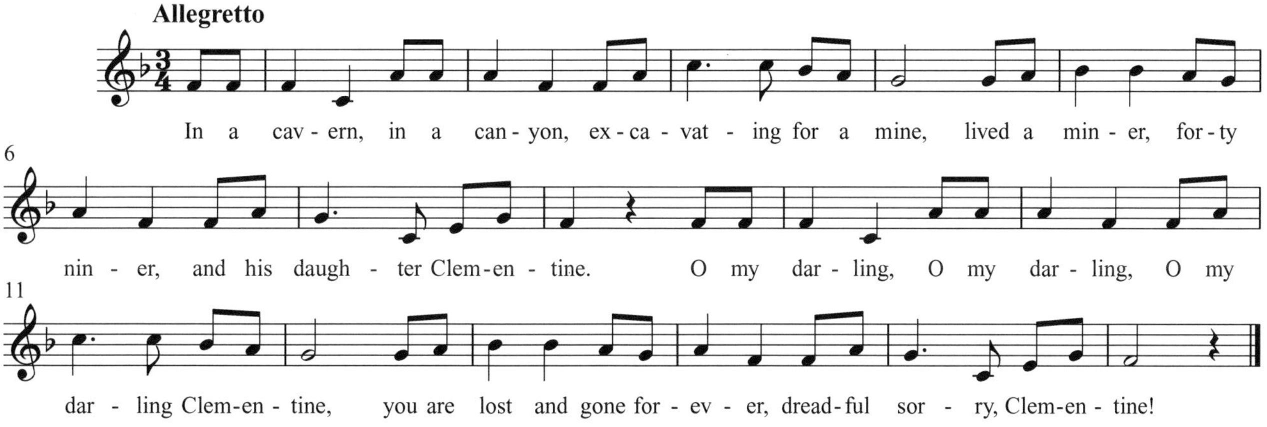

O Shenandoah

Ten Thousand Miles

For Further Study

To properly learn to conduct, one needs to study with an experienced master teacher with whom one can develop the correct skills over time. There are numerous conducting texts on the market, some of them good and some not so useful. Many contain far too much information in an attempt to put into words things that are quite difficult to talk about, but much easier to demonstrate.

The standard text often cited for conductors is Max Rudolf's *The Grammar of Conducting* (Wadsworth Publishing, 3rd ed., 1995). A wonderful book for young conductors is Elizabeth Green's *The Modern Conductor* (new 7th ed., with Mark Gibson, Prentice Hall, 2004), although it does not give much information specific to conducting choirs. Relevant to the topics raised in this chapter from Prof. Green's book are Chapters Two and Four. Both books cited here, however, will help further explain the basic issues with conducting for the student who desires more written information.

Chapter Two

Two Hands

In Chapter One, we dealt with the physical skills required of the right hand. Traditionally, the right hand is the principal instrument for conveying tempo, meter, style, and articulation to your ensemble. The left hand is more concerned with cueing the choir and indicating dynamics or phrasing, cutoffs or releases, and is used for such mundane things as turning the pages of the score.

Training your right and left arms to be independent of each other is a slow process for most. Following are some exercises which will help. Use these in various combinations and practice them frequently until you feel that, no matter what your left hand is doing, the pattern you are conducting in your right hand does not change or falter. Keep bounce and weight in the beat pattern, maintaining a level conducting plane.[1]

A clear ictus point is vital to creating clean ensemble singing.

The Left Hand

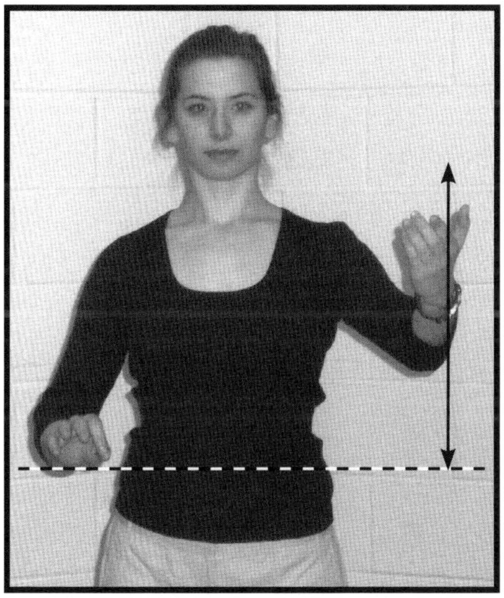

First, some exercises that will help you achieve the independence of your right and left hands and arms. While conducting a four pattern in a moderately slow tempo:

1. Raise your left hand from waist level to chin level over the course of four beats, and then lower it over the course of four more beats. Do not vary or disrupt the pattern in your right hand, or allow the left hand's movement to be bumpy and uneven. Make your left arm move in a smooth, steady gesture from your waist to your chin and then back down again. It may help to stop conducting patterns in your right arm for a bit and just move your left arm on its own a few times (much as you separate your hands in piano practice

[1] I strongly advocate the continuing use of the bounce patterns presented in Chapter One. Conducting that is more legato in nature is easy to assimilate, attained by simple modifications of these patterns. But it is essential that young conductors have a clear ictus point in their gesture at all times. In my experience, students who move too quickly to a legato-style conducting pattern develop sweeping gestures without these clear ictuses. While experienced professional choirs may not always require ictuses to sing together, less-experienced ensembles undoubtedly will.

to teach them to work independently). Similarly, stop moving your left arm briefly and just work with your right-hand pattern before attempting both hands together again. It is helpful to work in front of a mirror or with a partner so you get feedback.

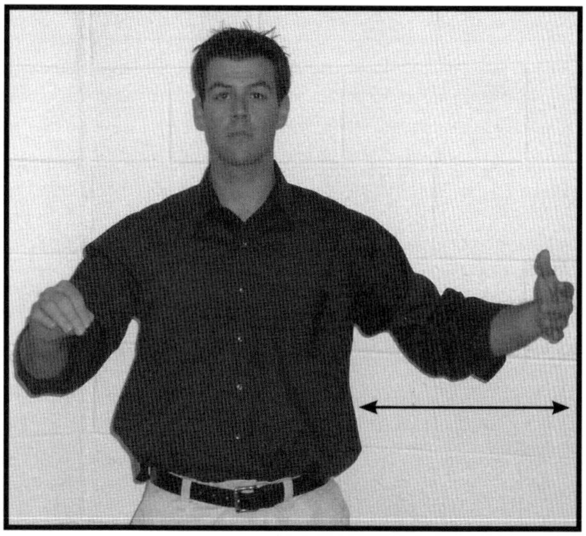

2. When you are comfortable moving your left arm up and down over one measure (four beats) and can do so without interfering with your right arm, then move it up and down over two measures.

3. When you have mastered moving your left hand up and down, try moving it from the center of your body outward, until your arm is outstretched from your body. As before, move it outward over the course of four beats and then back over the course of four beats. Keep the left-hand motion smooth and even, and keep the pattern in the right hand clear, on an even plane. Keep weight in the beat. When you have mastered moving in and out over one measure (four beats), change to moving it over two measures. Again, you may find it easier to practice each arm separately before using them together.

4. After you have mastered both movements at a slow tempo in four, try them at a faster tempo. You may also change meters to three, five, or six. Consider moving your hand up and down or outward and back over the course of less than a measure or over the course of several measures. The idea, in the end, is for your left hand to be able to move independent of the right.

5. Need more practice? Try the childhood game of rubbing your stomach and patting your head at the same time! When you can do that, reverse your hands (if the right hand was the "stomach rubber" at first, assign that task to the left hand).

6. For more advanced practice, make a circle with the left hand while conducting a pattern with the right; or conduct a pattern of four in the right hand, and two in the left hand.

Starting, Cueing, and Stopping

The key to clear communication lies in controlling the speed of the rebound.

Conductors often talk about cueing, and undoubtedly you are aware of what that term means. But if one thinks only to cue—a mistake often made by young conductors—the task will be undertaken too late to influence the music. A better way of thinking about this task is to consider the cue a preparatory beat. If you remember that you have to prepare the sopranos to enter on the third beat, for example, you will mentally be in the right spot to give them information in time. In other words, your prep or cue gestures need to dictate the "how" of performance, not solely the "when." If the cue comes as the sopranos are singing their entrance on the third beat, it is too late to show them how they should sing their line. If you want to prepare an entrance on the third beat of a measure, for example, you must give the musical information before that ictus if the cue is to carry any meaning. If your cue is on the ictus, you are already behind the game. The same idea is true for fermatas and cutoffs, which require the same before-the-fact preparation.

Think of this another way. Suppose you are a tour guide, leading a group of people through a dark cave. Would you wait for someone to hit her head on low-hanging stalactite? No. You would warn her ahead of time that around the next bend was a low-hanging rock that could cause her harm. So it is in conducting: lead your ensemble through the piece by preparing them ahead of time for difficult entrances, hidden themes, and so forth. Cueing them as they are executing something, rather than before they do it, is akin to letting them bang their heads on the rock!

Because, like cueing, starting and stopping are largely about communicating information, all three conducting tasks share some common traits. Foremost among them: In communicating ideas and information to your ensemble, the time that is most important is the rebound immediately preceding the ictus where you want something to happen. You should recall from the first chapter the observation that, while ensembles live on each ictus, conductors live in the rebound. And the important rebound for you is always the one preceding the ictus, as it is the only time that you can impart information to your singers or players. After all, if you want someone to begin on the downbeat of a measure, you must give him the preceding beat if he is to sing on time. Inherent in this logic are two factors: the preparatory beat must be 1) in tempo and 2) in the character of the music. The first factor will be addressed in this chapter, and the second in the next.

Cues are really preparatory beats.

Another common trait is eye contact. Vital to all effective conducting, eye contact is never as important as when starting, stopping, or cueing. Preparatory beats, cues, and cutoffs will only work properly if you maintain consistent, meaningful eye contact with your ensemble. It is necessary also to breathe with your choir when they breathe. You do not need to fake a large breath—breathe with them naturally. Empathizing with their physical task and participating in it with them is crucial to getting them to do things together, and to coordinating their efforts with your gesture. Finally, because humans can judge the speed and distance of vertical (up/down) motion much more easily than motion with depth (forward/backward), it is important that all preparatory gestures maintain some degree of a vertical axis if they are to be read effectively and instantaneously by your ensemble.

Cueing a downbeat

Starting voices that begin singing on the first beat of a measure is the simplest preparatory beat. Conductors commonly refer to this type of cue as a preparatory gesture, and it is one with which you will all be familiar. One of the easiest ways to learn this, and any cue, is to mirror your right-hand conducting pattern with your left hand.[2] Begin by simply mirroring each of the three basic patterns (two, three, and four) until you feel comfortable, watching yourself in a mirror or working with a partner to get feedback on what you look like to your ensemble.

Then, move on to cueing an entrance that begins on the downbeat of a $\frac{3}{4}$ measure. Start by conducting a three pattern in your right hand. When that is comfortable, add the left hand (mirroring) on only the third beat of the measure and the subsequent downbeat. The third beat, then, becomes the preparatory beat for the action you want to happen, specifically the choir's entrance that takes place on the first beat of the next bar.

---

[2] Some teachers warn against mirroring, but a quick glance at professionals shows that they mirror a great deal. While you do not want to mirror all the time in your conducting, it is not inherently bad unless you do so constantly to the detriment of other musical information you could be indicating with your left hand.

Conduct for several minutes in this fashion, with the right hand conducting a three pattern and the left hand conducting only on beats three and one. When the left hand is not conducting, it should rest either at your side or at the conducting plane, coming into motion only on the two beats in question.

It is much easier to judge vertical motion than motion which comes directly at us.

Once your hands feel comfortable doing these movements, begin to give the left hand more freedom by bringing it out of the mirroring pattern. Move it outside of the conducting box, visualizing that you are cueing various sections of your ensemble. Alternate cues in the direction of the sopranos, for example, with some to the tenors. When cueing, don't point at a section, but instead devise a hand gesture that, in effect, invites them to play or asks them to join the ensemble. Your role as conductor, remember, is that of leader and facilitator.

What you have just practiced now enables you to begin a piece that starts on a downbeat. The only difference is that your right hand won't be continuously beating in a pattern until after the work has started.

With every prep beat, you will make eye contact, breathe with the choir, and be in tempo.

Starting a work on the downbeat

To start a work on a downbeat, staying with our three pattern, let both hands mirror beats three and one together. It may help to count silently in your head the first two beats of the bar, letting the right hand begin conducting on only the third beat (and then continuing) and the left hand conducting only the third beat and ending on the first ictus of the next measure. Try the example following, singing it on "tah." It is most important to hear the music before you begin. The ability to hear the music before you conduct it is crucial to developing good communication with your group.

Cueing on a beat other than the downbeat

In preparing an entrance on a beat other than the first one, the concept is the same. In order for someone to begin playing or singing on any beat, you must prepare them on the preceding beat (remembering to breathe with them!). In cueing on the second beat, then, as in the example below, you should begin by conducting a continuous three pattern in the right hand. When that feels comfortable, mirror with the left hand (in the pattern) the first and second beats only. Do not conduct the third beat with the left hand, but let it rest either at your side or let it relax at the level of the conducting plane.

Cue this way several times until both hands feel comfortable and retain their independence. Then take your left hand out of its mirror pattern and make it move independent of the right. Keep both hands slightly to the side of the body so they are out of each other's way. Now extend this exercise to other meters, using the examples on the facing page and others that you make up yourself. Begin your practice by cueing from a mirroring posture, and eventually make the left hand cue without mirroring the right-hand pattern.

The preparatory beat should always be in the exact tempo of the music to follow. If done properly, a single, full preparatory beat is adequate to start an ensemble—you should not need to conduct a full measure of music, or even two or three beats prior, in order to get your ensemble to start together. If the music begins on a portion of a beat, however, as in the example below, you may need to give a full beat before the partial beat in order to allow your ensemble enough time to prepare to play or sing.

Practice cueing on each beat of a two pattern, then a three pattern, then a four pattern. When you have mastered all conceivable cues in these common patterns, then practice cueing in other meters (five, six, seven, nine) and in subdivided patterns of two, three, and four. In a subdivided meter, depending on tempo, you may not need to give an entire beat before a cue. If the tempo is fairly slow, you may only need to cue a half-beat before the entrance you want to affect. In the end, you should be able to start a piece on any beat of a measure in any meter.[3]

Ask a couple of friends to clap beats according to your cues. Having someone give you a physical reaction is a good way to test whether your gestures are clear.

3 See page 27 for a number of exercises you may use to further practice these skills.

An alternate way

Since most initial preparatory beats move up and down—and since musicians are very familiar with this gesture as the starting one—it is possible to use this up and down motion for all cues and preparatory beats that begin a passage or section of music, rather than having the left hand mirror the right.

When cueing on the third beat of a measure of 4/4, for example, conduct the full beat before by moving up and down, as if you were cueing a phrase that begins on a downbeat. But instead of moving to one in your pattern, conduct beats three and four. In other words, conduct an upbeat on the second beat (breathing with the choir). Then, instead of going on to a downbeat, move to where three would normally be in your conducting pattern. The only consideration is that you must remember to resume conducting in the appropriate place in the right-hand pattern. Here is an example for practice:

This method of cueing is easier in many ways, and often clearer to your ensemble. But it comes with the same caveat: cues and other preparatory beats need to occupy one full beat before the activity, and with this method of cueing it is easy to rush the preparatory gesture.

Right-hand cues

There are often instances where you will want to cue with your right hand instead of your left. You may want to use right-hand cues when your left hand is cueing someone else, or when your left hand is dealing with matters of style (phrasing, articulation, dynamics), or when the direction of the cue dictates that a right-hand cue might be more physically comfortable or easier.

Cueing with the right hand is quite easy. The right hand simply comes out of the beat pattern for an instant to cue the entrance, and then returns to the pattern. Practice doing this, varying both the meter and the beat you are cueing.

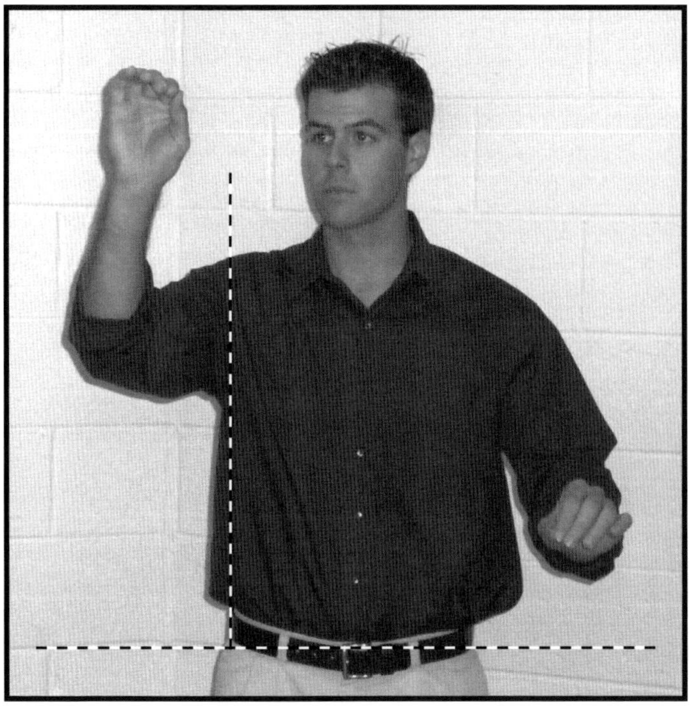

Cutoffs and Fermatas

Cutoffs

Cutoffs by themselves (without fermatas) are much like cues: the purpose is to indicate a point of action—in this case, where to stop singing—by giving an ictus point. There is no need to get complicated, and in fact doing so can hinder your objective. A simple ictus point is all your performers need in order to know the exact point in time at which sound should cease. Remember that cutoff/release gestures must also be prepared. You need to give your singers a full-beat warning that they have a task to perform: telling them where to cease singing is no different than telling them where to start singing.

You should practice cutoff gestures within the context of the piece. In the simple example below (which can be sung on "tah"), practice cutting off the second voice with your left hand while the top voice continues its melodic line. Be careful that the right hand, which is keeping a steady, weighted beat, is not influenced by the left-hand gesture.

Fermatas

Fermatas are a bit trickier, but they are based on the same concept as preparatory gestures. There are three types of fermatas:

1. Fermatas that have a distinct break followed by a short silence and a breath before continuing; and ending fermatas, which are similarly conducted.
2. Fermatas where the cutoff also indicates a breath and is the preparatory gesture to continue.
3. Fermatas that stop the music, but then continue without a breath.

When conducting each of these fermatas, remember that in order to get the choir singing again, you should breathe with them on the preparatory beat. Meaningful eye contact is also essential at all times.

The first type of fermata is the easiest, and it has two elements: a hold, best done without motion, and a cutoff. The cutoff may also function as a preparatory beat for the next phrase of music. Let us use this example, sung on "tah":

Conduct the first three beats as normal. On the fourth beat, give an ictus point, but do not give a rebound, since a rebound indicates renewed activity on the following beat. Hold the fermata without motion, then give a preparatory beat in the tempo of the piece (or perhaps even a little bit slower) and end with a clean ictus point, again lacking in rebound; as illustrated on the next page.

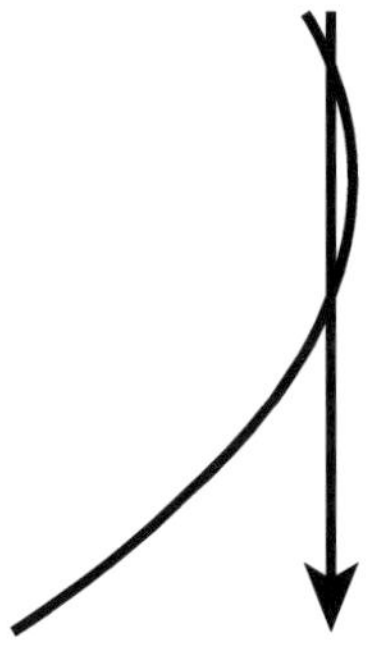

The ensemble needs only the exact point in time in which they are to cease activity. Avoid big circles or other flamboyant gestures, which only obscure this ictus point. There will be plenty of opportunity to play the maestro later, when you have developed clarity. For right now, a simple up and down gesture will suffice.

Allow for a moment of hesitation (the *caesura*, or railroad tracks). Then give another preparatory beat (in essence re-articulating the fourth beat), and then continue on by conducting normally in the second measure.

Conducting an ending fermata is exactly the same, except that there is no need to prep the choir to continue singing further music. In this instance, conduct the ictus of the fermata note without a rebound; hold the fermata; then give a preparatory beat to cut off the sound, using a simple, clear ictus point to indicate the final cutoff.

The second type of fermata, where the cutoff gesture also functions as the preparatory beat to continue, is perhaps the most common.

Conduct a brief fermata where indicated. For the cutoff, give a preparatory beat that not only indicates a clear ictus for the cutoff, but one that has sufficient rebound to indicate that the next beat follows immediately. You have several gestures to perform: the hold on the fourth beat; the preparatory beat for the cutoff; a rebound upwards; and, in tempo, the new downbeat of the second measure.

In the third type of fermata, there is no cutoff. For this type, an example of which is shown below, you would hold the fermata as above. Then, without giving a definitive starting point (which will make your choir stop singing), ease into the preparatory gesture for the new downbeat in such a way that your ensemble will sing without breathing. In this instance, the left hand may be very helpful in indicating to the choir to continue singing without taking a breath.

The skills presented here for cueing and for conducting cutoffs and fermatas should be practiced until you are comfortable executing them. As with all conducting gestures, these need to become a natural part of your musical expression. When you speak, you do not have to think of the words you want to use; your thoughts usually form mentally before you open your mouth (at least that is the hope). In conducting, then, you want your gestures to follow naturally from your musical impulses. This will happen with dedicated practice and concentration, in front of a mirror to start, and later in front of an ensemble.

Use the Bach chorale that follows to help practice fermatas. When practicing this, make sure you choose to use each type of fermata gesture at least once.

O Sacred Head, Now Wounded

SATB, ***a cappella*** **J.S. Bach (1685–1750)**

Two Other Helpful Gestures

The Click Beat

Often, a conductor will need to give a beat that impels quicker action than a normal ictus point, what I call a click beat. Examples of when to use this gesture include an entrance on a partial beat or at a syncopated rhythm, as in these two instances:

A click beat is easy to perform: it is an ictus point that has a particularly rapid rebound, often followed by a short hesitation in the pattern. Think of throwing a dart, or throwing a small pebble into a pond to make ripples. This specialty beat is quite useful in many situations, and is a good one to make sure you have in your repertory. If done correctly, you may think of it as kicking your choir off the beat and into the syncopated or off-beat rhythm.[4]

The Hitch Beat

There is another gesture that is very useful to have in your repertory, sometimes called a hitch beat. It involves a very slight pause at the top of the rebound (the hitch), which adds a bit of extra time to a rebound, allowing singers a quick breathing space without stopping the music.

In the following example from Mozart, the singers are required in m. 8 (the second measure shown) to sing a loud high note, immediately followed by a lower, *sotto voce* passage. The string players need to make a similar drastic dynamic change, and they have even less time to adjust. The object of the hitch beat is to allow everyone the very briefest of moments to accomplish this task—in effect, the music breathes along with the singers.

Lacrimosa (*from Requeim*)

SATB with piano **W.A. Mozart (1756–1791)**

To accomplish the hitch, move through the measure in the four pattern, rebounding on the fourth beat exactly in tempo. Stop for less than a beat at the top of the rebound—this is the hitch—and then proceed in tempo to the downbeat of the next measure. The hitch at the top of the fourth rebound will look something like the photo at the top of the next page.

---

[4] A short video clip demonstrating the click beat is provided on www.conductingchoirs.com, the companion website to this text series.

The hitch beat is easier to execute than to describe.[5] The key is to stay in tempo both on the rebound upwards, and on the prep beat downwards. The hitch itself is a short, suspended moment—somewhat akin to the moment at the top of the roller coaster, just before the long drop!

Further Practice

Following are examples for use in practicing cue and preparatory gestures. In these, cue each beat marked with an arrow. You may practice these alone, or a friend may "tah" the rhythms, failing to "tah" if you give an inadequate cue.

[5] To aid in the descriptive process of the hitch beat, a short video clip of it in practice is provided on this book's companion website.

Use the next example, from choral literature, for further practice in cueing.

Sing Ye Muses

SATB with piano **John Blow (1649–1708)**

For Further Study

Both the Rudolf and Green texts cited in Chapter One contain further information on the topics covered here. Chapter 8 ("Conducting Patterns and Choral Gestures") in Wilhelm Ehmann's *Choral Directing* (Augsburg Press, 1968) is carefully written and very helpful. Abraham Kaplan's *Choral Conducting* (W.W. Norton, 1985) is also recommended, particularly Chapter 3 ("Tempo Fluctuation, Left Hand") and Chapter 4 ("More About Conducting Patterns").

Chapter Three

Expressing Ideas

Music lives and breathes by countless subtle differences in the shape of phrases, inflection of pitch, and slight variations of rhythm, dynamic, or articulation. It is important that young conductors learn early how to make conducting gestures that are expressive, emotional, and meaningful. Too often inexperienced conductors (and even some experienced ones) concentrate too much on the "when" of conducting—cueing this entrance, giving that cutoff, preparing this beat—and forget about the "how" of making music. How should this phrase be sung? How should this pitch be inflected? No quarter note is the same as any other. If all the black dots were created equally, then computers would make better music than humans.

Conducting expressively is not important only at the end of the process, during a performance. Expressive conducting is also necessary in rehearsals. The more effective and communicative your gesture is early on, the quicker you will be able to convey ideas to your ensemble, and the less time you will need to talk them through each expressive detail you think the music demands.

Pattern Character: Articulation and Style

Until now, we have been working on the technical basics of conducting and coordinating the left and right hands as they fulfill different functions. Now, it is time to practice ways to reflect the character of the music being performed.

Musical character—the mood or effect that a passage of music evokes—might be defined with appropriate adjectives describing the drama, the feelings, or the emotions that it contains. Such labels might include simple terms like legato or maestoso. Other descriptions might be more complicated or subjective, such as the label "sprightly" to describe the opening of Mozart's "Eine kleine Nachtmusik," or "foreboding" to describe the beginning of Verdi's Requiem.

The Right Hand

So how does one change the conducting gesture to better show music's constantly changing and evolving soundscape? Some means are simple. By way of example, think of alterations we can make to the basic four pattern we've learned. It is helpful to think of it as a marcato conducting style: one that requires a consistent, easily readable ictus point. This is useful for music which is more heavily articulated or rhythmically active (like much Baroque music, for example).

With slight alterations from this marcato conducting style, we can make the right-hand pattern more legato by relaxing the rebound of the beat, or by making the pattern slightly more horizontal in nature. This de-emphasizes the ictus point, softening it and encouraging the ensemble to sing with more connection between notes.

Staccato conducting will require even quicker rebounds than marcato. Here, the rebound is not only short, but in some passages of music it may actually stop for just an instant between ictus points.

The Left Hand

The left hand may also be used for indicating expressive changes. Typically, the left hand might show accents (particularly *sforzandi)* with appropriate gestures. Remember that singers become quite adept at reading the speed of rebounds, and will respond appropriately. Also remember that we read vertical motion much better than movements with depth, and that it is the change of direction that indicates the ictus point. Therefore, make your accents a sharp, quick vertical drop and rebound upwards. Beware of gestures that don't rebound, or those that are horizontal, directed straight at the singers.

Indicating Dynamics

There is an old saw that the size of the conducting box (its outer dimensions) is directly related to dynamic. In other words, for *forte* passages use a large box, and for *piano* passages use a smaller one. While this certainly can work in some situations, it is not necessarily a good thing to rely upon. The size of the conducting box is primarily related to tempo. Want proof? Try to conduct a *fortissimo* passage in a very fast tempo. If you try to do this in a large box, you will look foolish! If the tempo is fast enough, you will be forced to use a smaller conducting box. Similarly, try to conduct a very slow piece at a *pianississimo* dynamic by making your conducting box very small. It will be difficult, because you have taken away from the box all the space you need for your slow rebound.

So what other means are available to indicate dynamic level? Several techniques follow, but I also strongly suggest that you watch what other conductors do and learn from them, as there are many, many ways to indicate dynamics.

For softer passages, try raising the conducting plane. Remember, too, that the conducting box is three-dimensional (horizontal space, vertical space, and depth). So for softer music, try moving the conducting box closer to your body. Similarly, for louder passages, move the plane lower or place the conducting box a little further from your body.

If the music gets louder, the conducting box can get broader or more horizontal. As music becomes more forceful, think of where you want your singers to produce that sound: not in their chests and necks, but in the center of their bodies. So put your conducting gestures in the same place, encouraging your choir to dig down into their breath-support mechanism.

It is very useful to think that music has tactile qualities—qualities that you can touch, feel, and hold. I often talk to my students about how much weight music carries, which is often the combined functions of dynamic and articulation. I ask them to think about how they might carry six bags of groceries, or what they would do to lift the piano off the ground. Those same gestures, postures, and stances are exactly what are needed to indicate more weight in a given musical passage.

Sometimes young conductors will indicate dynamics by raising or lowering their left arm to indicate a crescendo or decrescendo. This only works if the left hand does not end up too high, where it certainly doesn't look like it can hold much weight, or too low, where it cannot be seen. However, if you watch experienced conductors, they will rarely utilize this gesture. From the start, you, too, should find a better way to show dynamic changes.

Following are several musical examples of differing characters. For each example, devise a style of conducting that reflects the character of the music. For the first two examples, you might subtly alter the speed of the rebound: a little faster rebound can indicate a crisper ictus point. For "Ave verum corpus," slow the rebound: allow the ictus point to land gently, followed by legato, elegant rebounds. Conduct in front of a mirror or with a partner in order to get feedback. Be careful that your basic pattern does not lose the character of weight and centeredness that you worked so hard to obtain. Your legato should not lose its ictus points completely, nor should your marcato pattern become too brisk or flippant.

Drunken Sailor

Folksong

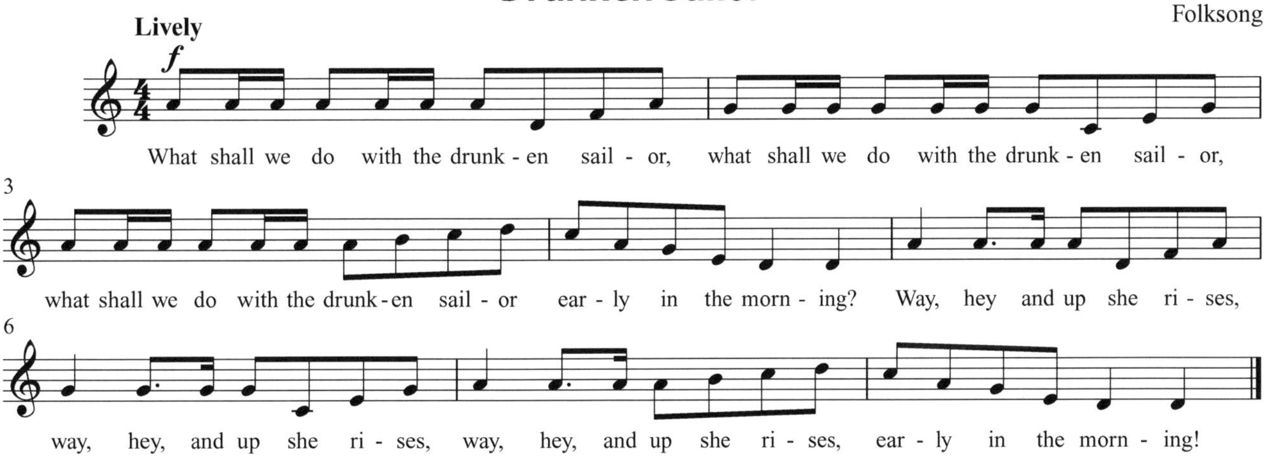

Chandos Anthem No. 4, Mvt. 6

SATB with piano

G.F. Handel (1685–1759)

4
of Him. Let the whole earth stand in awe of Him. Let the
awe of Him. stand in awe
awe of Him, stand in awe
awe of Him. Let the whole earth stand in awe of Him. Let the
8
whole earth stand in awe of Him, stand in awe of Him. Let the
stand in awe of
stand in awe of Him. Let the
whole earth stand in awe of Him, stand in awe of Him. Let the

11
whole earth, let the whole earth stand in awe of Him.
Him. Let the whole earth stand in awe of Him.
whole earth, the whole earth stand in
whole earth stand in awe of Him, stand in awe of Him, stand in

14
Let the whole earth stand in awe of Him, stand in awe of Him.
Let the whole earth stand in awe of Him, stand in awe of Him.
awe of Him, stand in awe of Him.
awe of Him, stand in awe of Him.

Ave verum corpus

SATB with piano **W.A. Mozart (1756–1791)**

9
Vir - gi - ne: ve - re pas - sum, im - mo -
Vir - gi - ne: ve - re pas - sum, im - mo -
Vir - gi - ne: ve - re pas - sum, im - mo -
Vir - gi - ne: ve - re pas - sum, im - mo -

14
la - tum in cru - ce pro ho - mi - ne;
la - tum in cru - ce pro ho - mi - ne;
la - tum in cru - ce pro ho - mi - ne;
la - tum in cru - ce pro ho - mi - ne;

Conducting Very Slow Tempos

Conducting slow tempos is more difficult than conducting brisker ones because controlling the speed of the rebound is harder. Not uncommonly, young conductors will try to fill in the time by either stopping the rebound completely, hesitating, and then continuing; or they will begin to conduct subdivisions of the beat in between the ictuses. Neither is a good idea. Learn to conduct a smooth, evenly paced rebound even in a very slow tempo. It may help to imagine conducting your pattern through water, as you work to add resistance to your hand and arm motion. If the tempo is extremely slow, try to imagine conducting through sand! Here are the opening few measures of Fauré's Requiem, which are very slow:

Requiem

SATB with organ **G. Fauré (1845–1924)**

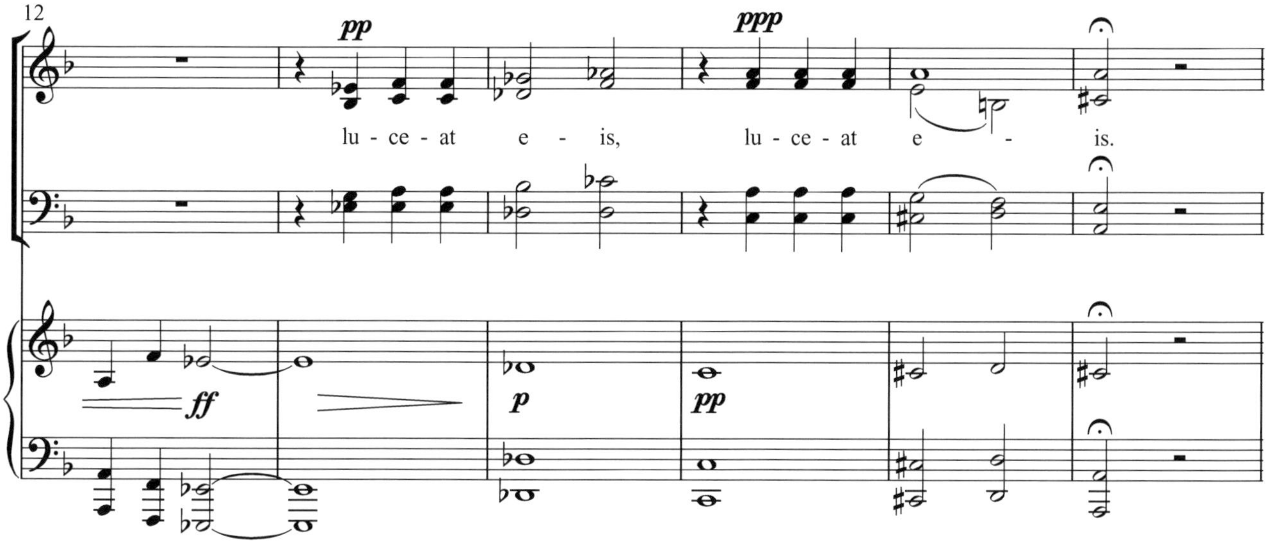

Changing Tempo

Conducting Rubato and Tempos that Slow

Two of your primary functions as a conductor are to keep a steady beat for your ensemble and to help with cues, articulation, and other means of shaping the music. Occasionally, music from certain style periods (the Romantic period, for example) or from certain genres (like opera arias) requires that you divest yourself of the function of time keeping and instead allow the music some give and take, some breathing room. Conducting rubato is not particularly difficult, and only requires some practice in order to do it with conviction.

When conducting rubato passages, always keep the metronome beat in mind. The principle of rubato is that one note is "robbed" (the literal translation of *rubato*) of part of its value, which is then attached to another note. The total amount of time in a measure should remain, in theory, relatively constant from measure to measure. Another way to think about this: remember that rubato doesn't always mean slowing down, but it sometimes means speeding up a bit. (Another rule of thumb: a little rubato often goes a long way!)

The key to controlling tempo lies in controlling the rebound and its speed.

Rubato conducting, as in *ritardando* and *rallentando* passages, requires slowing the tempo. This requires slowing the rebound of the pattern. It will do little good to make the ictus points more forceful without slowing the rebound: it is the speed of the rebound that your choir will read in order to judge where the next ictus will land. It is vital that you think of a subdivision of the meter while slowing (for example, think of sixteenth notes while conducting quarter notes). You will control the slowing of the beat pattern as the subdivision slows incrementally, and the tempo decrease will be perceived as occurring naturally within the phrase.

Two folksong examples that lend themselves to rubato conducting are provided at the top of the next page. Practice these examples first alone and silently, and then with a few friends singing. Repeat each example until your conducting gestures are clear and readily readable.

O Shenandoah

Ten Thousand Miles

Conducting Tempos that Speed Up

A similar but opposite technique of that for rubato is useful for conducting *stringendo* or *accelerando* passages. To speed up a passage, you need to increase the speed of your rebound. This may also, but not necessarily, require decreasing the vertical space of the rebound. To keep the increase in speed uniform, it is again helpful to think a subdivision of the beat. As that tempo increases incrementally, your beat pattern will also speed up in a natural, organic fashion. Two musical examples for you to practice are found on the next few pages. Again, practice first with the music in your head, and then practice with friends playing or singing. In *stringendo* passages, faster rebounds will be needed to increase the tempo, just as a slower rebound was used to achieve the opposite result.

I Love My Love

SATB, *a cappella*

G. Holst (1874–1934)

Huic ergo (from *Requiem*)

SATB with piano **G. Verdi (1813–1901)**

4
Come prima
er - go par - ce De - us,
par - ce De - us,
hu - ic er - go
hu - ic er - go par - ce
Come prima
7
f
par - ce, par - ce De - us.
par - ce De - us.
par - ce par - ce De - us.
De - us, hu - ic er - go par - ce De - us.

Metric Modulation

Metric modulation is a twentieth-century concept that you should understand. It entails a rhythmic shift where the underlying rhythmic value of one section of music equals a different rhythmic value in the new section. The principle actually has been around since the Renaissance, where it is referred to as the proportion. Found in large numbers of motets, the idea of proportion is tied to the recurring beat, or *tactus*. In today's musical language, the tactus is usually a half note in 2/2 or cut time which is equal to (takes the same time as) the dotted quarter note in an adjoining 3/4 section of music.

Examine any number of motets by Giovanni Gabrieli, Claudio Monteverdi, or another Renaissance or early Baroque composer and note the relationship between the sections in two and those in three. While the proportion is not always made explicit, these metrical shifts are common, and with experience you will recognize them and know how to execute meter changes such as those in the continuo from "Hodie completi sunt," by G. Gabrieli, that follows. In this example, the measure of 3/4 is equal to one beat of the 2/2, so that now two measures of the music in three take the same time as one measure of music in two.[1]

Metric modulation in contemporary music also uses a common denominator, where the rhythmic value of a new section of music is derived from a rhythmic value of the preceding section. (For instance, what was the subdivision of the beat becomes the beat itself, or vice versa.) In the example below, the eighth note of mm. 1–2 is equal to the eighth note of mm. 3–4, and the dotted quarter of mm. 3–4 travels at the same speed as the quarter note of the last measure.

In practical terms, you would mentally subdivide the beat in the first measure, thinking the eighth note while conducting in three. As you move to the meter change in the third measure, allow for three eighth notes where you had previously counted two (the beat of m. 3 is now 50% longer than the beat of m. 2). Reverse this procedure for the next transition: don't subdivide the final beat of m. 4, but count it as one beat and continue on by conducting in 4/4.

The metronome value of the beat changes as you do this. If the quarter note is MM=60 for the first measure, then each eighth note is traveling at 120 (60 x 2). Three of these constitute the beat of mm. 3–4, so 120 ÷ 3 = 40, the pulse of the dotted-quarter note. Since the beat of measure four now equals the beat of measure five, the tempo of the quarter note in the last measure also equals 40. You can see how a composer, through notation, can change the tempo of a piece so that you, as a conductor, know exactly what the metronome value is at any time.

---

1 Read the proportion entry in a music dictionary or similar reference source for additional information and clarification.

Conducting the Music

Your goal is to learn to conduct the ideas and emotions in the music, not beat patterns at your choir.

The end goal of your conducting study (whether you end with one course or whether you continue on with graduate study, with master teachers on your own, or through workshops and conferences), should be to conduct the ideas inherent in music.

Conducting is more than keeping time. It is a gestural technique that allows you to communicate ideas to your ensemble, as well as the execution of those ideas. You have undoubtedly watched professional conductors who conduct differently than you have learned here, and who may sometimes seem unclear in their patterns or difficult to follow. And yet, these conductors make music at the highest level. Why? Because they have discovered what the composer's intentions were, they have formed ideas about how to get those intentions across to an audience, and they have been able to arouse the interest of their ensemble in working together to communicate those ideas. As well, conductors who work with top professionals can sometimes work without what we have presented as basic information (like beat patterns that are always perfectly straightforward) because the music they are performing is well known by the singers or players, and they have worked so closely together over a long period of time that the ensemble understands the conductor's gestures and knows how to read them.

Of course, the foregoing is hardly an excuse for you not to have the best, clearest gestural technique that you can. The clearer you can be with your hands and arms, and the more information you can convey through your technique, the less time you will have to waste in rehearsal communicating those ideas with words or demonstrations.

Your principal job as a conductor is to communicate ideas through the medium of sound. Your gesture is the most important aspect of that communication, and something you must master, but it is not the end result. Music is the end result. This will now be our focus: learning ways to analyze music that allow you to discover a composer's intentions—why he chose to write what he did—and fashioning rehearsal techniques that allow you to impart those ideas to your choir in a succinct fashion.

For Further Study

Two excellent readings will enhance the material covered in this chapter. In Elizabeth Green's *The Modern Conductor,* cited earlier, read Chapter 10, "Melding and the Virtuoso Technique." Jameson Marvin wrote a marvelous chapter, "The Conductor's Process," in *Five Centuries of Choral Music: Essays in Honor of Howard Swan* (Pendragon Press, 1988). While this festschrift may be a little difficult to locate, the reader will be well rewarded for his or her effort.

"Developing Expressive Conducting Techniques," Chapter 5 in Lewis Gordon's *Choral Director's Rehearsal and Performance Guide* (Parker Publishing, 1989) will repay study. And a large portion of Abe Kaplan's *Choral Conducti*ng, cited in the previous chapter, is applicable to the concepts presented here.

Chapter Four

Repertory and Programming

Among the roles conductors have is to program music for their ensemble to perform. The music the choir sings—its quality, genre, and difficulty level—will determine not only if they are successful on the upcoming concert, but also whether, over the long term, they continue to learn new skills and to develop and grow as singers and musicians.

Finding Literature

In order to run a successful school, community, church, or professional choir, you need to know vast amounts of choral literature. A principal key to success lies in programming appropriate music for your choir:

- Music that is challenging, yet not so difficult that the choir cannot be successful when performing it
- Music of a wide variety, from all periods and all genres of choral literature
- A quality of literature that enables you to teach important skills and that allows the choir to grow and learn

Too often, sadly, conductors fall into common traps. They either program music that they already know and have performed before, or they are too eager to program only new music that is sent from music publishers each year. Selecting repertory takes study and care: finding exactly the right pieces for your ensemble is a time-consuming task, but one that lies at the foundation of a successful program. Having recourse to or knowledge of hundreds of pieces of music is essential to your survival. Think not just of how many works you may need to program one season for your ensemble, but of how many concerts you will conduct with them over the next ten, twenty, or thirty years of your career—then multiply that by how many different choirs you will conduct each year. You begin to see the magnitude of the effort.

Here are some guidelines for finding literature for your choirs:

- Music publishers produce each year an enormous amount of new music. Some of it is quite fine, and some of it is not. Remember that publishers are in the business of making money, and that fact may be at odds with your musical goals. That said, take what you can from their catalogs and use it; but don't rush to your music dealer each fall, snatch up copies of all the latest things, and decide that your job is complete.

Selecting repertory takes time, study, and care.

Publishers sometimes offer to send you sample copies of new music. Take advantage of their generosity and write to them asking for copies of those pieces you like. Keep these copies in a file, and refer to them each time you start to program a new concert or a new season. You may also browse online, and publishers' catalogs there increasingly feature musical clips of their octavos.

- Be involved with professional societies. Organizations like the American Choral Directors Association, Chorus America, the International Federation for Choral Music, and the Music Educators National Conference hold periodic meetings at the state, regional, and national levels. Each features several (or many) choral ensembles, selected to appear by audition from among their peers. Not only will you hear wonderful groups, but you will hear many pieces of unfamiliar literature, usually with publication information in the program. Make notes on which might be useful for your choir, then contact the publisher and secure copies of them for your files.

  These conferences also have music publishers and music dealers among their exhibitors. What an excellent opportunity to browse new editions and old standards, and to purchase—or be given—single copies for your reference files! You will also find valuable information on their websites. Don't forget online communities, either, such as Choralnet.org.

- Attend other choral concerts. Extra time is hardly plentiful for most busy professionals, and nearly every conductor has concerts at similar times of the year, it seems (at the holidays, near the end of the school year). However, the opportunity to hear choirs similar to your own is invaluable. Make time to hear these groups, not only to support them and hear what they are doing, but to hear what literature they may be performing that may also work for your groups.

- Meet and talk to your peers at conferences, district and regional chorus festivals, honor choir concerts, and similar events. They are struggling to find the right literature as much as you are, and the opportunity to share new pieces at these times can be very useful.

- Go to music dealers. Many, particularly larger firms, have large inventories of choral music in stock. Spend an afternoon browsing and looking through their files. Purchase single copies for your files to refer to later.

- Finally, do not ignore the choral music library in your own school or church. You will find many great pieces there. Do not be put off because a work is older and may exist in yellowed, dog-eared copies buried in the back of a shelf: One of these pieces may be just the one you have been looking for!

Programming Objectives

When programming and choosing repertory for your ensembles, whether school groups or adult choirs, there are a number of long-term objectives to keep in mind. During the time a singer spends in your choir, he or she should be exposed to as wide a range of literature as possible. Singing music of many diverse kinds enables both individual singers and choirs to develop the musical skills, listening habits, and vocal resources needed meet the performance demands that each style or type of music requires.

The vocal skills needed to sing a Baroque motet are different than those required for a Britten part song; so, too, are the listening skills and musical/stylistic nuances. If the goal is to develop a well-rounded, flexible ensemble, then performing a diverse musical program is essential. Similarly, in an educational setting, if the goal is to inform your students of the history and treasures of choral literature through their performance of its masterpieces, then it is obvious that they must sing some of all of this literature. To work towards these goals:

Allow your singers to explore the rich and varied tradition of our choral heritage.

- Program music from all epochs of music history, from the Renaissance until the present day. You do not necessarily need to program something from each period each season. If a student sings in your choir for three years of high school, for example, then during the course of those three years she should have sung at least some literature from each historical period, either in the large ensemble, a chamber choir, girls' chorus, or other specialty group.

- Program both accompanied and unaccompanied literature, noting that accompanied music should include not only music with piano, but with other instruments as well (brass ensembles, string quartets, organ, wind ensemble). The literature for choirs is vast—far larger than for any other performance area, since choral literature extends into the past two or three hundred years further than the standard repertory for voice, orchestra or band, or opera.

- Perform music from a variety of styles. The majority of your music should be classical—after all, this is why choirs as performing ensembles were begun, and it is the tradition to which we belong. But choral literature is also rich in the traditions of folksong arrangements, spirituals, and more recently, vocal jazz. There is a similar choral tradition in opera and musical theatre, and literature from those genres is also appropriate for your choir. Popular music has almost no choral tradition, and as such it should probably have a limited role in any choral program.

- Program both sacred and secular music. In a school music program, one does not have to advocate a religious purpose for singing sacred music. It is enough that some of the most creative minds in human history have written for choir (Bach, Mozart, Haydn, Brahms), and these vital cultural artifacts deserve to be learned by your choirs and heard by your audiences, regardless of the textual source. It is difficult to imagine that an administrator or parent would complain about a one-on-one experience between a student and one of Michelangelo's masterpieces, yet these are all on sacred subjects. There is really little basis for objecting to the study and performance of sacred music when such study is based on cultural rather than religious grounds.

- Finally, program music for a variety of voicings. Your choirs should not only sing four-part mixed choral music, but eight-part (or more), as well as music for single-gender choirs (SSA or TTBB). The rich vein of music written for these groups should be explored, and the experience of singing them should not be denied your singers.[1]

Putting It Together

"Art isn't easy," argued Stephen Sondheim in *Sunday in the Park with George*, and that includes the art of programming. Knowing hundreds of choral pieces is one thing, but constructing a good concert program is even thornier. I have attended too many concerts where

[1] A short bibliography of repertory guides that may assist you in finding music begins on page 52.

Structure a concert program like you would a good meal, and don't only choose desserts!

the conductor simply programs 12 or 14 pieces in a row, without concern for how they go together. There should be a flow and an order to a concert program, much like there is to a meal. A good meal starts with something small, like a salad, before you get to the main course, which is accompanied by vegetables. And dessert, while important, is something to be savored at the end of the meal. To continue the metaphor: the salad and vegetables of a concert are its shorter, serious pieces, while the main course is a longer piece or one more complex for audiences to grasp and for singers to execute. The dessert of a concert, its folksongs or spirituals, should not be its focal point. Doing lighter literature is both acceptable and necessary, and indeed this body of music is one of the most beloved of our choral heritage, but its performance should not come at the expense of more substantial music.

Programming does not need to be the most challenging intellectual exercise. It is enough that there should be a good reason that two or three numbers are grouped together. Often, that reason is simple: a grouping of three opera choruses; two Handel choruses; three nineteenth-century part songs; and so forth.

A "Typical" Choral Concert

There are many types of programs, but let's begin with what I term a typical choral concert. This is similar to those that I use when touring with my university Concert Choir, because it allows us to sing a wide variety of music in many different styles. Something valuable for us to do, hopefully it also contains at least some music of interest to each audience member.

I begin such a program with a short, upbeat number. Not only does this provide a celebratory opening to the concert, but it also serves to focus audience attention and rewards their anticipation of the concert with a brief piece. I have used various genres of music for this, from Baroque motets to new, commissioned works.

The first segment of the program is usually historic and often consists of three Renaissance motets. I think of a through line for these pieces: three motets that

West Chester University Concert Choir
California Tour Program

Gottfried Homilius		Deo dicamus gratias
	I	
Hans Leo Hassler		Dixit Maria
Marc Antonio Ingegneri		Tenebrae factae sunt
Jacob Handl		Pater noster
	II	
J.S. Bach		Komm, Jesu, komm
	III	
Michael White		Goin' Home on a Cloud
arr. René Clausen		Simple Gifts
Robert Ray		He Never Failed Me Yet
	Intermission	
	IV	
Music from West Chester		
Samuel Barber		Reincarnations
		Mary Hynes
		Anthony O'Daly
		The Coolin
Robert Maggio		Jacklight
	V	
David Conte		Charm Me Asleep
Dominick Argento		In Praise of Apollo

follow the chronological order of the church year, for example. I arrange them in a tempo scheme that allows for variety (fast/slow/fast, for instance). This section of the program is fairly meaty in that the works are serious, usually sacred, and from a time period that is increasingly unfamiliar to audiences. However, because the works are usually comparatively brief, the audience's concentration is not overly taxed.

Following these pieces is a longer work, which is usually the most difficult work in the first half of the program. Often, this is a motet by Bach or Brahms, or two pieces each six to eight minutes long that can co-exist musically and textually (though not necessarily from the same musical epoch). This section requires more attentiveness and concentration from the audience, but by this point in the concert, they should have been prepared for the intellectual concentration required. The first half of the program usually ends with two or three "dessert" pieces, often spirituals, since the first half of my tour programs is nearly always comprised of sacred music.

I follow a similar pattern in programming the second half of the concert, which is most often devoted to secular music. I begin after the intermission with three or four shorter, more contemporary works, followed by a longer work that is more difficult. The concert ends with lighter music, such as the two selections from the California Tour Program shown on the facing page, as the first half concluded with folksongs and spirituals.

Once you have programmed this concert—culling all of your resources for appropriate literature—put it aside. This allows time to think about alternate pieces, substitute new ones into the program that may have escaped your attention earlier, etc. Later, return to the program and think about its impact:

- Is there a wide variety of music, from several periods, genres, and styles?
- Do the tempos of the pieces vary, or have you programmed too much slow or too much fast music, and is the pace balanced throughout the concert?
- Is there dynamic contrast between the selections in a set, and throughout the program?
- Do the key relationships make sense? Is the tonal area within each group varied? Three pieces in a row, all in G major, is not good. Neither is a group where the keys of each piece bear no relationship to one another. Try to arrange different works so that the tonal areas make a logical progression from one to another, or at least complement each other (for example, three motets that move in progressive steps along the circle of fifths, like G, A, and B major; or which stay in flat key areas, like E flat, C major, then A flat).

After asking these questions, make adjustments where necessary, and then consider the new concert order. Eventually, you will arrive at what you think will be a good concert, challenging to your choir, but one they can sing successfully—and one interesting to your audience.

The Otterbein College Early Music Ensemble
Music of War and Anguish

	I
Giuseppe Marini	Gite, sospiri
	II
J. P. Rameau	Laboravi clamans
M.A. Charpentier	Chorus Damnatorum *(Extremum Dei judicium)*
Clement Jannequin	La guerre
	III
Orlando Gibbons	I Tremble Not at Noise of War
G. F. Handel	War, He Sung, is Toil and Trouble *(Alexander's Feast)*
	My Strength Is from the Living God *(Samson)*
	O Fatal Day! *(Saul)*
	IV
C. Monteverdi	Introduzione e Ballo "Movete al mio bel suon"

Themed Concerts

There are other ways to program a concert, too. The most prominent of these is the theme concert. These are quite common, and can center around a time of the year ("A French Christmas"), an historical period ("Music of the Thirty Years War"), a season ("Music for Spring"), or an idea ("Music for a Time of Pestilence," a concert I once gave that combined reflective Renaissance motets and AIDS poetry that the choir members recited). The list is endless and is limited only by your imagination, knowledge, and desire to investigate new repertory.

Finding music for your choirs to sing and programming it appropriately is difficult and time consuming. What is often hardest is that, until you have considerable experience, you will not know if the literature works together and the program is well constructed until you have lived with it for a while and performed it for an audience. Younger conductors could seek out a more experienced mentor who might take time to look over a proposed program and make suggestions. With time, however, you will be able to make better choices and know earlier in the process how those choices will be received by choir and audience alike. The foundation for challenging your singers, enticing them to exciting music making, and building a healthy choral program lies on a solid knowledge of the vast and glorious repertoire of our choral heritage.

For Further Study

Repertory Guides: A Short Bibliography

Anderson, Linda Allen. *The Foundation of Artistry: An Annotated Bibliography of Distinctive Choral Literature for High School Mixed Choirs.* Oklahoma City: American Choral Directors Association, 2002.

Bloesch, Richard J. and Weyburn Wasson. *An Annotated Bibliography of Twentieth Century Choral Music Appropriate for College and University Choirs.* Oklahoma City: American Choral Directors Association, 1997.

Bullock, William J. *Bach's Cantatas Requiring Limited Resources: A Guide to Editions.* Lanham, MD: University Press of America, 1984.

DeVenney, David P. *American Choral Music Since 1920: An Annotated Guide.* Metuchen, NJ: Scarecrow Press, 1993.

__________. *American Masses and Requiems: A Descriptive Guide.* Metuchen, NJ: Scarecrow Press, 1990.

__________. *Early American Choral Music: An Annotated Guide.* Metuchen, NJ: Scarecrow Press, 1988.

__________. *Nineteenth-century American Music: An Annotated Guide.* Metuchen, NJ: Scarecrow Press, 1987.

__________.*Varied Carols: A Survey of American Choral Literature.* Westport, CT: Greenwood Publishing, 1999.

__________ and Craig R. Johnson. *The Chorus in Opera: A Guide to the Repertory.* Metuchen, NJ: Scarecrow Press, 1993.

Green, Jonathan D. *A Conductor's Guide to Choral-Orchestral Works: Part I.* Metuchen, NJ: Scarecrow Press, 1994.

__________. *A Conductor's Guide to Choral-Orchestral Works: Classical Period, Volume I: Haydn and Mozart.* Metuchen, NJ, 2001.

__________. *A Conductor's Guide to Choral-Orchestral Works: Twentieth-Century: Part II: The Music of Rachmaninov through Penderecki.* Metuchen, NJ: Scarecrow Press, 1998.

__________. *A Conductor's Guide to the Choral-Orchestral Works of J. S. Bach.* Metuchen, NJ: Scarecrow Press, 2000.

Hawkins, Margaret B., et al. *An Annotated Inventory of Distinctive Choral Literature for Performance at the High School Level.* Oklahoma City: American Choral Directors Association, 1976.

Locke, Arthur Ware and Charles K. Fassett. *Selected List of Choruses for Women's Voices.* Northampton, MA: Smith College, 1964.

Research Memorandum Series of the American Choral Foundation, published by Chorus America. This long series, begun decades ago, contains nearly 200 bibliographies to the music of various composers, genres, epochs, etc. A full list of titles may be found on the Chorus America website (www.chorusamerica.org) and copies of individual issues may be ordered there.

Roberts, Kenneth. *A Checklist of Twentieth-Century Choral Music for Male Voices.* Detroit: Information Coordinators, 1970.

Schmidt, Sandefur. *Music Performed at American Choral Directors Association Conventions 1960–2000.* Oklahoma City: American Choral Directors Association, 2002.

Strimple, Nick. *Choral Music in the Twentieth Century.* Portland, OR: Amadeus Press, 2002.

Wachsmuth, Karen. *A Bibliography of Twentieth-Century Hungarian Choral Music.* Oklahoma City: American Choral Directors Association, 2002.

Choral Music History: Four Sources

Jacobs, Arthur, ed. *Choral Music.* New York: Penguin Books, 1963

Shrock, Dennis. *Choral Repertoire.* Oxford University Press, 2009.

Ulrich, Homer. *A Survey of Choral Music.* Wadsworth Publishing, 1973.

Young, Percy. *The Choral Tradition.* New York: W.W. Norton, 1962, 1981.

Chapter Five

The Score and the Rehearsal

The ability to conduct well is directly related to the level of understanding of a musical score. One can have a beautiful, fluid conducting technique, yet have little to say with it. Learning what to say—by undertaking a thorough analysis of the score—is a musician's most critical function, and the prime ingredient to successful conducting. A strong musical vision well informed by detailed analysis is also important because the conductor is expected to forge a single musical impulse from a disparate group of musicians, many of whom may also hold strong ideas about the music they are performing.

Here also lies a trap. One of the most dangerous words in a musician's lexicon is interpretation, as in, "I will now show you my interpretation of this work by Mozart." Too often, this use implies that the speaker has some ideas about what the music means to him or her, and that these ideas are about to be imposed upon the score.

That is a flawed approach to what it means to interpret music. A much better concept, and one that captures the conductor's responsibility, is to speak of understanding the score in question. Understanding what Mozart, or Bach, or Beethoven, or Stravinsky had in mind is the first step towards realizing it in performance. Music is about ideas—it says things that words cannot—and good musicians seek out those ideas that lie embedded in the score, underneath the surface of the notation.

Music is about ideas and emotions—musical notation is only a crude way of representing these.

A thorough analysis—with the goal of understanding the composer's intentions—also allows the conductor to make rehearsal and performance decisions that will communicate his understanding to an audience. We can never know what Bach, Mozart, or Stravinsky really intends in a composition; we can only guess at it. Even when a composer is alive, there are limits to what he or she can tell us about any particular score (if they could tell us in words, there wouldn't be any reason to write the music, would there?). With time, patience, maturity, and reflection, we can come perhaps very close to a composer's intentions. The method presented in this chapter should prepare you in your quest to understand a composer's ideas, and give you ways to translate that understanding to your ensemble, and through them to an audience.

The Choral Score

Choral scores are usually straightforward: the highest sounding voice part normally appears at the top of the page and the lowest sounding appears at the bottom. Most choral scores present the singers' parts on separate staves, often with either a piano reduction of the parts (if the piece is unaccompanied) or a piano accompaniment (which may be a reduction of the orchestral parts in a major choral work).

It is important to notice that the tenor part is written in treble clef (often, but not always, with an accompanying *ottava* sign). There are many other choral scorings: SAB, SSATB, SSA, TTB, etc. Publishers often choose to score a piece combining more than one voice part to a staff, thereby allowing more music on each page. Many church anthems, in particular, are scored SA on one staff and TB on the other. In these situations, the tenor part is written in the bass clef. Major choral-orchestral works present the most challenge to the choral conductor: one not only needs to know the choral scoring, but also the accompanying instrumental parts, and their relationship to each other. In all situations, the conductor must clearly know the score in order to navigate the assembled forces toward the final product.

Choral scoring has changed through the centuries. The use of C clefs, usually a different one for each voice part, predominated until well into the nineteenth century, before the present two-clef system came into wider use. Nearly all of the choral music written in the Renaissance period existed in part books, where a singer would only see his part when performing a particular piece.

Today, the normal choral voicing for adult, mixed choirs is four parts, two for the women's voices (higher and lower) and two for the men. In the Renaissance period and into the early Baroque era, a five-voice choral score was common: SSATB, with three parts for the upper voices. Since many of these scores, especially in sacred music, were written to be performed by boys' voices and because pitch was generally lower than today, the women's voices did not necessarily overwhelm the men's. One will find this voicing used in secular compositions (madrigals, for instance) as well, which most likely did include adult women singers.

In music literature for today's middle school singers, it is common to find three-part mixed or SAB music, where the ranges are kept within a limited parameter appropriate for young voices. Because this music is sung by unchanged boys' voices, it is common for them to sing any of these three parts (and, occasionally, for a girl to sing the "baritone" part). For this reason, many composers and publishers will designate these parts as simply I, II, and III.

Analysis for Conductors

Analyzing a work from a conductor's standpoint is somewhat different than looking at a work as you might have in music theory class, in part because you are seeking slightly different results. In music theory, your questions sought mostly to understand the techniques a composer used in order to create the score:

- What key is the work in and where does it modulate?
- What is the form of the work?
- What are its melodic or rhythmic motives?
- How has the composer orchestrated the work, and to what ends?

Those questions remain the same when approaching a score as a conductor, but you must answer additional questions, including:

- What does this information mean? When performing this work, how will these facts affect your interpretive decisions?
- Where are the dramatic or emotional climaxes in the work, and how will knowledge of these moments affect your performance?
- How will the mechanics of the score as you have uncovered them help you to rehearse this work better or more efficiently?
- Where are the conducting problems in the score (problems of balance, tricky transitions, difficult ensemble spots), and how will you solve them?
- Where are the vocal challenges, those places that may be difficult for your singers to sing?

Structure is content. What a piece means is directly linked to its musical grammar.

My students learn and live the mantra, "structure is content." By this I mean that what a piece of music means—its message, its emotional and intellectual content—is inseparable from its composition. Composers choose to write music in a certain way, carefully choosing harmonies, melodies, rhythms, tonal relationships, and so forth. In the same way that the meaning of a story or a novel cannot be divorced from the way that it is written—the words the author chose, the sentences she constructed from them, and the paragraphs and chapters that are created—a piece of music cannot be separated from its grammar and syntax. In other words, it is how the elements of music (pitch, rhythm, harmony, meter, timbre, texture, and structure) combine that elicits emotion and meaning.

Our Ethical Responsibilities

As musicians, we have an obligation to the music that we perform and to the human beings who created it. This can get lost in the process of re-creating musical masterpieces. I've sometimes posed the following question to my students when, in conducting class, they try to impose their own feelings or their will on a work.

Suppose that you had lots of money and a Monet water lily painting came on the market for sale. You decided that you would really like to have it, so spent the $50 million or more to purchase it. You take it home and put it in the place of honor over your sofa. You love the painting, but after a few days of looking at it, you decide that the pink colors in the painting don't really go with the sofa. You decide that you are going to fix that to make a more harmonious color scheme in your living room. Your investment aside, do you have the right to take a little green paint and "touch up" Monet's work so that it better fits in with your furniture?

While you may have the legal right as the owner of the painting, Monet's works are some of the masterpieces of Western art, and most people understand that you have no moral right to ruin one of them for future generations. We have a responsibility to carry forward those cultural artifacts that help define us as a civilization.

In the same way, we do not have the right to alter a work by Beethoven, Bach, Mozart, or anyone else. Before the mid-twentieth century, performers often re-touched or re-orchestrated composers' works, but we have since come to understand that this is an aberration. The works by these composers and others like them are the musical and artistic patrimony of some of the most creative minds in Western music. It is our job as performers to bring them to life as close to the wishes of the composer as we can come. While that may be a difficult task, it is nonetheless essential. We do not have the right to impose ad hoc our will, our thoughts, or our feelings onto a musical work. To do so is not ethically responsible.

The guidelines for analysis that follow are intended to help you discover a composer's intentions. They are designed to help you gain insight into the musical and structural techniques that composers use to embody ideas, thoughts, and emotions in a score.

A Procedure for Analysis

Setting up expectations

Before you begin your formal analysis of the work, it is important to have a set of expectations—what you might expect to find in your study of the piece. (If you don't know what to expect, how will you know if what you find upsets your expectations, that it is something important, or out of the ordinary?) It is often helpful, if not essential, to do background reading on the composer or even the specific work you are going to analyze.

Having done so, take a moment to browse through the score and reflect on these or similar questions:

- Does the piece look simple or complex? Why do you think so (lots of black on the page, many accidentals, several meter changes, etc.)?
- In what key is the work? If the composer changes keys, to where might he modulate? If the work is from the common-practice period (roughly the years 1750–1930), what tonal areas might you expect to find as related or contrasting key centers?
- From the title or the opening lines of text, what character might you expect to find in the music (anger, solemnity, passion, humor, etc.)? How might that character be demonstrated in the music?
- From which historical period is the work? What performance practices, harmonic language, or other stylistic characteristics would you expect to find in this work that it might share in common with similar pieces from the same period?
- What do you know about this composer? What might you expect to find in this work in common with other works you know by this composer?
- What do you know about the author of the text? What might you expect to find in this text, recalling others by this poet you might know? If the text is liturgical (a mass movement, for example), what other music do you know that sets the same text, and might you expect the composer to treat the text similarly in the piece you are studying?

Analyzing the work

After you have answered the above questions, you are ready to undertake a complete melodic, harmonic, rhythmic, and structural analysis of the work.

1. Do a complete harmonic analysis of the work. If the music is from the common-practice period, this needs to include a chord-by-chord harmonic analysis, including identification of non-harmonic tones. If the work is from the Renaissance or earlier, it should include a

thematic analysis of the work, identification of points of imitation, suspensions and other non-harmonic tones, and so forth. Twentieth-century analysis may encompass yet different methods, including identifying tone rows or other non-traditional scalar constructions. You should also determine the harmonic rhythm: do the harmonies change every quarter note, every half note, once a measure? The harmonic rhythm of a piece is a very important measure of how fast information is being sent out to the listener.

2. Do a complete melodic analysis of the work. What short motives does the composer write, and how are they used or changed over the course of the movement or the work? Is there repetition of longer melodic fragments or complete melodies, and do those mutate over the course of the work? If the work is polythematic, trace the use and development of each theme in each movement of the work. Do individual movements share melodic material with earlier or later movements?

3. Undertake a rhythmic analysis of the work. Are there rhythmic motives that unify the composition? Do these change over the course of the movement or work? Are there motives shared by various movements or sections of a longer work? In Renaissance or earlier music, note unusual or irregular rhythmic groups (groups of three pulses in duple meter, for example).

4. Chart the orchestration of the work. Where are the strings used? The brass? The woodwinds? If it is purely a choral work, where does the composer use only the men's voices, for instance, or reduce the musical fabric from four voices to two or one?

5. Only now are you ready to define the architectural structure of the composition.[1] How does the composer create form in this piece? Is the form a common one (sonata, rondo, theme and variations, fugue), and if so, does it deviate in any significant ways from what you might expect in similar compositions from this composer or from this era in music history? Which structural elements provide unity to the composition, and which provide contrast?

6. Decipher the structure and content of the text. How does the composer treat the text: are there elements of text painting, for instance? How does the musical structure of the work relate to the textual structure? Where are the important images in the text, and how are they treated musically? Where is the textual climax, and does it correspond to the musical climax?

Drawing conclusions

After you have analyzed the work, ask yourself:

- What did you find that is salient, interesting, or unexpected (in the context of the time in which the piece was written, both theoretically and historically speaking)? Consider harmony, melody, rhythm, form, text, and other basic elements of music.

- What key areas are established and how? How do they relate one to another (length of time a tonal area predominates, pitch relationships between them, and so forth)?

[1] I strongly recommend waiting until you have gathered your evidence before defining form in music. If you decide from the outset that a piece is in sonata form, chances are you will find that form in your work, whether it exists or not. Instead, play detective: gather all the clues, amass all the evidence, and only then solve the puzzle.

- How does the composer employ his or her forces? Does the manner in which the composer uses the forces (chooses timbre) contribute towards its structure? Are certain instruments related to thematic ideas in the text or the music?

- How does the meter or pulse change, and to what purpose? What is the effect on mood, emotion, and character?

- How are dynamics used to provide melodic or rhythmic interest, contrast of texture, or to help create form?

- How does the composer employ timbre or tone-color changes? How does the orchestration contribute to the structure of the piece? How does timbre help convey drama, emotion, or meaning?

- What are the micro and macro formal characteristics or structure of the work? Make a chart showing graphically all the information you have discovered during your score study, like this one of the "Lacrimosa" from Mozart's Requiem:

Form:	Sectional				
Section:	a	a'	a" Transition	a"'	Coda
Smallest phrases:	1–2 3–4 5–8	9–10 11–14	15–20 21	22–23 24–28	29–30
Larger phrasing:	8 (2+2+4)	6 (2+4)	7(6+1)	9 (2+5+2)	
Key:	d	d	mod.→F d	d	
Forces:	str, cho +brass, ww/str	cho, ww/str +brass	cho, str +brass + ww	tutti	
Text:	"lacrimosa..."	"lacrimosa..."	"Huic ergo..."	"Dona eis..."	"Amen."

- Make decisions now on phrase structure and breathing based on what you have found in your analysis. Mark these in your score.

- At any given moment in a piece of music, the composer is usually moving towards or away from a dramatic moment. Where are the dramatic/emotional highlights of this work? How does the composer approach them and then leave them? Identify these points not only for the whole composition, but also in its constituent sections.

- Identify the primary motivating factors in the score: what moves the music forward at any given moment, or impedes its forward momentum at other times? These might include harmonic movement, rhythmic motion, or melodic themes or motives. They might also include orchestration choices, dynamic changes, or tempo variations.

- What expectations does the composer set up for the listener and how are they fulfilled or not?

An Analysis Example

The Kyrie from Haydn's *Little Organ Mass* is provided on the following three pages. I encourage you to analyze it according to the questioning process outlined above. Then, compare it to my analysis of the work, which begins on page 64.

Kyrie (from *Missa St. Joannis de Deo*)

SATB with piano

F.J. Haydn (1732–1809)

9
lei - son, Ky - ri - e e - lei -
p
lei - son,
lei - son,
Ky - ri - e e - lei -
p
lei - son, Ky - ri - e e - lei -
11
son.
f
son. Chri - ste e - lei - son, e - lei - son,
son.
f
14
Chri - ste e - lei - son, Chri - ste e - lei - son, e - lei - son, e - lei - son.
p

17
Ky - ri - e e - lei - son, e - lei - son, Ky - ri - e, Ky - ri - e e -
20
lei - son, e - lei - son,
lei - son, e - lei - son,
Ky - ri - e, Ky - ri - e e -
lei - son, e - lei - son,
23
lei - son, e - le - i - son.

Setting up expectations

Does the work look simple or complex?

After a brief glance at the score, I would say the work looks relatively simple: the choral parts are almost always homophonic, and the accompaniment seems straightforward, comprised of chords articulated as sixteenth notes. A lack of accidentals leads me to suspect that the harmonic language will also be less complex.

In what key is the work?

The movement is in B-flat major. Because it is a work from the Classical era, if it modulates I would expect it to move to the dominant key (F major) or perhaps the subdominant (E-flat major). It might also move to the relative minor (D minor) or the parallel minor (B-flat minor).

What character do I expect to find in the music?

Because this is a setting of the Kyrie text, I will expect to find music of a somber character, perhaps with a note of pleading or even melancholy.

What formal, harmonic, or structural characteristics do I expect to find in this piece, in comparison with others like it?

Because of its era and composer, I would expect that the harmonic language used in the piece would be functional—that it would follow the procedures of the common-practice period. I further expect that it will be in a recognizable formal structure (sonata principle, rondo, rounded binary, or other such form). The work may further be bound together by recurring melodic or rhythmic motives.

How does this work compare to other works by Haydn?

I would expect that, like much of Haydn's sacred music, this mass movement would be relatively conservative in nature. It will probably lack some of the drama of his symphonies or the operatic influences of his later, larger masses. However, it may share some of the intimacy of his chamber music, since this is also conceived on a smaller scale.

Analyzing the work

1. Do a complete harmonic analysis of the work, being sure to note the harmonic rhythm.

After undertaking a harmonic analysis of the work, I discovered that the first 11 measures of the work reveal nothing unexpected. The root movement goes from tonic to dominant (in m. 5), then modulates to the dominant (F major, mm. 6–7), approached through its secondary dominant (C major). The music remains in the dominant key through m. 12. In m. 13, I discovered a color chord: a B-flat minor triad in second inversion. This flat tonic chord, outside the harmonic realm of F major, is joined in mm. 13–14 by F minor and D minor triads that lead to the secondary dominant (G major) of C major—the dominant key of F, where Haydn has briefly modulated. Mm. 15–16 prepare for the return of B-flat major, by means of an E-flat major triad and an F dominant seventh chord. B-flat major is then firmly established in m. 17 on the downbeat. We remain in this key for the rest of the movement, with standard cadential formulas of IV–V–I in mm. 20, 21, and 24 and a V–I cadence in m. 23.

The harmonic rhythm of the movement is fairly steady: usually one chord change per quarter note. This provides a stately harmonic progression. Only near the end (mm. 21–22) does the harmonic motion elongate to two or four beats of the same harmony. By slowing the harmonic motion at this point, Haydn brings the movement to its conclusion.

2. Do a complete melodic analysis of the work.

There are no melodic motives in this work, but it is unified through the use of a returning melody (mm. 1–2, and mm.17–18). Haydn's melodic motion is overwhelmingly stepwise, although the leap of a fourth occurs in m. 5 and the drop of an octave in m. 12. The melodic compass for each voice is in an easy range: for the sopranos, a ninth (F to G); for the altos and tenors the range of a seventh (C to B-flat for the altos, A to G for the tenors); and for the basses, a tenth (B-flat to D).

3. Do a rhythmic analysis of the work.

The rhythmic character of the work is tied to the declamation of the word "Kyrie," and is frequently set by Haydn using a dotted eighth/sixteenth/quarter note pattern. In four instances (mm. 1, 8, 17, 20) this is augmented into a dotted quarter/eighth/quarter idea. Both rhythmic patterns function as unifying devices for the movement. Haydn further unifies the work through the sixteenth-note articulation of the chord changes in the accompaniment.

4. Chart the orchestration of the work.[2]

Haydn's Kyrie is accompanied by two violin parts, cello, and continuo throughout. The orchestration is simple: the choir sings (doubled by the instruments), then the orchestra introduces new material. Thereafter, these two ideas are combined by Haydn. The choir always sings as a whole; there is no passage for women's voices alone, for instance. Nor does any voice drop out of the piece, even for a limited time. The instrumental forces play continuously, as well. Therefore, in this example at least, orchestration (the use of timbre) is not a structural element, and since it does not contributed to structure, I can conclude that it will not play a large part in conveying the emotion and meaning of the music. (Since orchestration is not a structural force, it is not placed on the structural table shown on the next page.)

5. Define the work's formal structure.

Based upon what I have discovered thus far, I am ready now to label the formal structure of the Kyrie as ABA'. This form is defined primarily by two means: the structure of the text ("Kyrie" for the two outside sections, and "Christe eleison" for the middle one) and by harmonic means (B-flat major predominates in the outer sections, while the middle section is mostly in F major). The form is further defined by the repetition of the initial melody repeated at m. 17.

---

[2] The example reproduced on pages 61–63 uses a piano-accompanied version of Haydn's Kyrie, making this portion of the exercise a challenge to complete. My analysis is based on my experience with the work, and I should note also that works with instrumental accompaniment should be conducted using a full score.

6. Decipher the structure and content of the text.

The text is structured by the return of the "Kyrie" text after the "Christe eleison" section. Haydn repeats words outside their normal usage in the Catholic liturgy (which has three repetitions of "Kyrie eleison," three of "Christe eleison," and then three more of "Kyrie eleison"). While this can serve to emphasize words for the purposes of text painting, here I do not believe that is the case. Instead, I believe that Haydn has repeated portions of the text for musical reasons, in effect using the text to help fashion the musical phrase.

Drawing conclusions

What did I find that is interesting or salient about Haydn's mass movement?

In my opinion, what drives the music forward primarily is its phrase structure. The initial two-measure phrase is followed by a longer phrase that is split into three short choral bursts, where the primary musical material lies in the accompaniment and the choral portions occur on the third beats of mm. 4 and 5, rather than on the first beats. This is in turn followed by a much longer four-measure phrase (mm. 7–10). The irregularity of this forward motion, driven in part by its harmonic content, is Haydn's way of creating drama—perhaps portraying the pleading of the congregation. The middle section is slightly more regular in its phrase groupings (two measures, then one, then three), but the harmony is more far-ranging, which adds to its feeling of angst. The A' section is similar to the opening, except that here the first two-measure phrase lacks the instrumental space after it, and the repeated choral "Kyries" intrude immediately, further underpinning the urgency of the pleading.

The climax of the movement comes in mm. 19–20, at the moment of the two, high "Kyrie" exclamations. Shortly after this (mm. 21–22) is when Haydn slows the harmonic motion, leading us to the conclusion of the movement. There are secondary climaxes at the downbeat of m. 8 (near the end of the opening section), and at m. 15 (at the same point in the B section).

Here is my structural chart for the movement:

Form:	A	Transition	B	A'
Smallest Phrases:	1–2 3–6 7–10	11	12–13 14 15–16	17–18 19–21 22–23 24–25
Larger Phrasing:	10 (2+4+4)	1	5 (2+1+2)	9 (2+3+2+2)
Key:	B-flat F			B-flat
Text:	"Kyrie..."		"Christe..."	"Kyrie..."

Finally, I will make some decisions for performing the piece. I have identified stress marks for each phrase so that each has a clear point where motion moves towards and away from. (I have added these on the score itself, as tenuto markings). I think a *poco ritardando* is needed on the fourth beat of m. 16, as Haydn approaches the return of the opening material. This also helps to set up the absence of motion when the sixteenth-note figure disappears from the accompaniment. It further clarifies the structure of the piece. There should also be a ritardando at the end of the work, coinciding with the choir's final "eleison," and a very brief fermata on the "-son," to give weight to the ending of the movement, reinforcing the feeling of conclusion.

Your Analysis and Rehearsal Planning

The analysis process just explained will help you find insights into the work you are conducting, enabling you to discover the ideas and emotions embedded in the score. The drawing-conclusions questions, in particular, should help you reach decisions about your performance choices: when you know how the elements of music combine in a given piece to create syntax and meaning, you should be able to more clearly ascertain which of those elements needs your attention at any given moment in order to communicate to an audience what the composer intends.

The final step in this process entails devising a rehearsal process that allows you to reach your performance choices. To do this:

- Locate difficult spots, likely passages that will present problems for your ensemble in terms of range, tessitura, ensemble, tough rhythmic passages, and so forth. It might be a good idea to create vocal exercises for use as warm-ups that address some of these tricky passages (high phrases on bright vowels, for example).

- Rank from most difficult to least difficult the various sections of the work. A rule of thumb: in general, tackle the more difficult passages in rehearsal first, saving the easier ones for later in the learning process.

- Then devise a plan that, given a finite amount of rehearsal time, will allow you to maximize the use of that time in order to rehearse the piece. You need not rehearse a piece of music from start to finish. Often, it is a much better use of time to rehearse different sections out of order, putting them in context together at a later rehearsal time.

- Rehearse organically: take apart the music and put it back together in the same way that the composer has. You don't necessarily have to start at the beginning of a work, but always work in complete phrases, combining adjacent phrases until you have a complete sub-section or section of the piece. Then combine two sections to make up a longer portion of the piece.

- Always link portions of the piece you have learned to new passages. Keep layering the music back and forth, being careful not to always stop at the same seams in the musical fabric. By doing this, you will build a strong foundation for your ensemble, a framework that organically reinforces the structure of the piece. In this way, they will learn not only the pitches and rhythms, but the grammar of the piece. Keep in mind the dictum, "structure is content"—how a work is put together is inseparable from its message and emotion.

Your rehearsal design should enable you to teach a piece so your ensemble will understand its musical, emotional, and dramatic content. How you go about that will include creative solutions to problems you expect to encounter in rehearsal. Experience and trial and error will help you a great deal as you conduct and rehearse more.

Hierarchy of needs in the rehearsal

III: Emotion and Meaning

II: Dynamics, Phrasing, Articulation, Ensemble

I: Pitches, Rhythms, Tempo, Text (possibly)

An illustration of the hierarchy of needs in a rehearsal is shown above. Rehearsals should begin at the bottom of the pyramid. Teach pitches and rhythms first, attaching them to the text as soon as possible. And remember that the music is not learned until all three musical elements can be performed at the correct tempo. When your ensemble has fairly well accommodated the demands of Level I, then begin to layer the elements of Level II into the musical fabric. Only when all of these elements combine in a satisfactory way can you proceed to Level III, and begin to discover the meaning that lies behind the notation.

Attention spans are getting shorter. When planning rehearsals, vary the pace and work in brief periods of time for younger groups.

Ensembles, particularly young ones, must have a context in which to dig deeper into the music. It will not do to begin work on a new piece with a ten-minute lecture on the composer and his or her place in history. That information is useful, of course, but it needs to come after your choir understands and knows the music itself. Paradoxically, the conductor must begin at Level III even at the first rehearsal. If you do not know what the music is about in all of its particulars, if you do not understand exactly how each phrase (and indeed each note) will sound in the final product, and how the work must function as a whole, then you are not ready to begin. Knowing this information will profoundly affect how you introduce the work to your ensemble at their first reading.

Preparing for the First Rehearsal

To ensure you are thoroughly prepared for the first rehearsal, proceed through the following checklist.

- ❑ Sing through each part, one section at a time, noting difficult passages where the choir may have trouble. Mark these, either in the music or on a rehearsal sheet you can refer to handily.

- ❑ Go through each section of the piece indicating phrasing and breathing places. Sing each phrase to make sure that you have not given the singers impossible phrase lengths, unless you want to employ staggered breathing.

- ❑ Having sung each part and determined phrase lengths (on a musical/textual basis, with musical reasons always taking precedence if there is a conflict), find an appropriate tempo based on: (in descending order of importance):

- Stylistic and musical considerations; if the composer has indicated a metronome marking, then you must have compelling reasons to alter it significantly
- Difficult passages that cannot be taken too fast or too slowly
- The ability level of the choir
- The tempo relationships between movements or sections of a work
- The acoustical considerations of the performance hall

❑ At this point, you should have very clear ideas about dynamic levels. Clarify these and write them in the score, particularly if the composer (any before the Romantic period) has not provided them in detail. Keep in mind the balance between and among the voices, and important thematic material that should be heard at a given moment. Remember as well to address any role dynamics play in formal design.

❑ It may be helpful, now that you have formed your own ideas about the piece, to listen to several recordings of it or to play it on the piano. Re-think all of your ideas and make modifications where you think they may be appropriate. I would caution you about relying on recordings for learning music you will conduct. It is perhaps the least effective tool for learning a piece of music. Far better for you to sing each part and play the score at the piano, because doing so is an active rather than a passive process. In addition, most choral music has not been recorded; if you come to rely exclusively on listening to a work before conducting it, what will you do when confronted with a piece you cannot listen to first?

Don't rely on recordings. Most choral works have never been recorded, so you must have some other method to draw upon when learning new scores.

❑ You may want to practice conducting the composition in front of a mirror. Cue each part as it enters, as well as all important musical material (re-entry of principal themes, for example). Always relate your gestures to the sound you want to hear, and fashion them in the character of the phrase that you are cueing.

The First Rehearsal

Things to do

❑ There is no overriding need to learn one whole piece when first reading it. Particularly if the work is long, choose a section of it to begin introducing the music to the ensemble. This need not be the opening of the work. It can be a portion from later in the piece, but it should be an organic portion of the score—a complete phrase, sub-section, or section from the overall formal structure. If the piece is in ABA form, then perhaps you will choose only to teach the music of the A section at the first rehearsal.

❑ If the chorus has good reading facility, try to let them sing without accompaniment. Not only is this a better way to learn, but it places the burden of responsibility for music making on the singers' shoulders.

❑ You may need to divorce the text from the music, particularly if the text is in a foreign language. Have your ensemble read the music on a neutral syllable, or with rhythmic chanting. However, if the text is easy but the rhythms are difficult, then reading the text with the correct rhythms, without the pitches, may be a very good way to begin.

❑ Remember that an immediate second reading of a section or a work may often fix many mistakes, simply because the singers now have a context for learning. Do not start breaking down the music right away; give your choir members a second chance to fix mistakes for themselves before you begin working on specific problems or working on separate voice parts.

❑ If the text is in a foreign language, teach it slowly:

- Pronounce it syllable by syllable for your choir, carefully and distinctly, having them repeat each after you.
- Then pronounce whole words, graduating to short phrases, and finally in complete sentences, always having the choir repeat the text after you.
- Provide your singers with a word-by-word translation of the text. It is best if you can give them both a literal translation and a poetic translation.
- Say the text in the musical rhythm of each part, at the correct tempo.
- Finally, sing the music with the text.

Things not to do

- Do not give a lecture on the composer and the background of the music. Introduce more of these remarks further along in the rehearsal process. Your ensemble does not need to know much about Mozart in order to learn the correct notes and rhythms of his music.
- Similarly, do not give a theoretical analysis of the piece before you have sung any of it. Talk about structure and meaning only when your ensemble has a context for understanding them—once they have lived with the music for a time.

Expression and articulation markings, dynamics, ritardandos, etc. are part of the score, not superfluous additions.

- Do not go through the piece or a section of it pointing out dynamics, expression marks, or changes of tempo. Not only does this waste valuable rehearsal time, it takes away the burden of responsibility from the ensemble. These markings are part of the music, not add-ons, and your choir members should get used to reading all of the information on the page, not only the pitch and rhythm notation. Furthermore, your conducting gesture should clarify these musical changes from the beginning of the rehearsal process, and singers should learn to follow not just the beat you are providing, but also the other information your gesture contains about style, articulation, and dynamic.
- Finally, do not automatically rehearse each voice part individually before asking everyone to keep working on the piece together. Not only does this leave half of the choir or more idle at a given moment, it disengages them from the rehearsal. Save individual practice for those times when you most need to break down the piece into smaller phrases, or for when your sopranos really do need to hear their part alone.

Score Marking

A rule of thumb to use in marking your score is the fewer marks the better. You should know the music well enough that you don't need to mark tempo changes, meter changes, or cues into the music. In other words, you should be able to read the score fluently without having to mark it heavily. Obviously, more experienced conductors may find this easier than those just starting out.

You will want to include some of the following in your score, however:

- Important cues, especially when they are buried in complicated passages.
- Principal themes when they recur after a long absence, or appear in unusual guises rhythmically or harmonically.
- Important structural or analytical information gleaned from your score study (such as where the development section of a sonata form begins, or where the composer modulates to an unusual key, or any other salient changes). Do include musical phrasing in your score. I usually put the larger phrase groupings at the very top of my page. For example, "10 (4+2+4)" where a new phrase grouping begins.
- A word-by-word English translation of any foreign text, so you know exactly what it means at all times.
- All articulations, dynamics, and breath markings that are not already indicated (especially in Baroque and Classical scores). These markings should also include for instrumental music any marks you may have placed in the players' parts, especially bowings for the strings. Mark all cuts and repeats clearly.

Numerous examples of common score markings for these and other elements are provided on the next page. In addition, many conductors use colored pencils or markers to help clarify the information in a score. You might choose yellow to highlight dynamic markings, green for important cues, pink for primary melodic material that should be heard at a given moment, blue for important secondary material, and so on. Particularly when dealing with larger or choral-orchestral scores, this can help to graphically show musical information in a way that marking things in pencil only cannot.

Common Score Markings

For Further Study

Two essays from *Choral Conducting: A Symposium* (ed. Harold A. Decker and Julius Herford, Prentice Hall, 1973) are very relevant here: "The Choral Conductor and the Rehearsal," by Lloyd Pfautsch (Chapter 2) and Julius Herford's "The Choral Conductor's Preparation of the Musical Score" (Chapter 5). Both are frequently cited in the literature on choral conducting and are standard readings for many undergraduate and graduate choral conducting seminars. Elizabeth Green's *The Conductor's Score* (Prentice Hall, 1985) is also valuable, although written from the orchestral musician's viewpoint.

Chapter Six

Singers and Choirs

The choral conductor must have a firm comprehension of the functioning vocal mechanism. Unlike the instrumental conductor who needs a basic knowledge of many instruments, the choral conductor deals with only one, the voice. But one should not operate under a false illusion: the vocal mechanism is not a simple device. The complicated workings of the voice are largely internal, unlike other musical instruments.

The Voice

It is the responsibility of the choral conductor to fully understand the singing voice and to be able to put that understanding to work in the rehearsal. Our discussion here will focus on three basic principles of vocal production: posture, breathing, and placement. It is clearly not within the confines of these writings to provide as complete a discussion as would be found in a volume intended for the future teacher of voice. Therefore, the choral conductor should seek as much intensive vocal training on the collegiate and post-collegiate levels as possible, and should also absorb as much of the excellent literature on the topic as is available.

Alignment (Posture)

Establishing good vocal posture is the first step in any choral rehearsal. The benefits of good posture are immediate. First, the lungs are able to fully expand upon inhalation, allowing for adequate breath for singing. Secondly, the body is in its proper alignment for singing, allowing it to function in the optimum manner for good vocal production. Singing is an intensely physical process; without an active, engaged posture, singers are encouraged to contribute passively to the musical product.

The features of good standing posture include the body weight being distributed evenly between both feet, the upper torso remaining upright and relaxed, and the head and neck in good vertical alignment over the hips. A good image for the sing-

ers is for them to feel like they are bouncing on the end of a diving board: indeed, try a few bounces before beginning other vocal exercises. When the singers hold their music, the folders need to be held comfortably high with both hands, and not at the waist, which encourages them to bend over (as well as takes their eyes off of the conductor).

Seated posture retains many of the same features, except that the feet are often better placed with one foot further in front than the other. In traditional chairs, the singers need to sit on the front of the chair with their backs straight and their weight forward. If modern posture chairs are used, the students can sit against the backs but in an upright manner.

Breathing

Correct breathing for singing is a crucial concept to teach early to a choir. Once proper posture has been established, the singer needs to open and relax the jaw and mouth comfortably, and then take a deep, silent, and low inhalation. The shoulders should remain still and relaxed throughout the breathing process. Done properly, the singer will feel expansion around the sides of the middle torso, the back, and in the abdominal area.

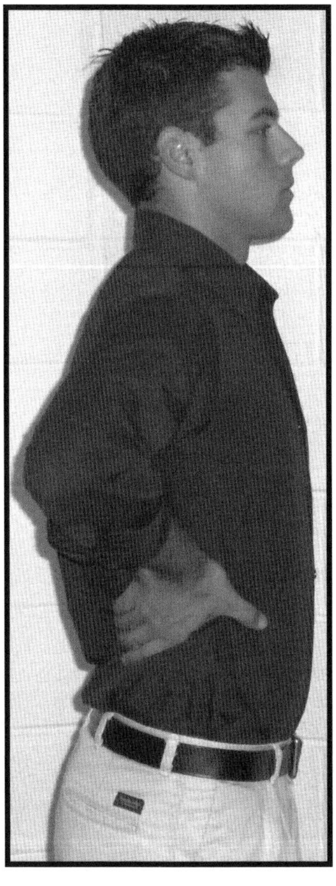

Breathing should not be a gasping affair. In fact, air pressure will do all the work for the singer to get a full breath. The simple fact is that when we have used most of our air and have reached the end of our lung capacity, the air pressure in our lungs is lower than the air pressure of the room. If one simply allows the rib cage to expand, releasing the muscle tension here, the air will rush into the lungs by itself. (Nature abhors a vacuum!) Conductors should guard against their singers gasping for air. Similarly, watch that they are not physically grabbing for a breath, perhaps by lifting their chests, craning their necks, moving their shoulders, or other such telltale physical signs. At all times while singing, the rib cage should be held upright, allowing the muscles of the rib cage (the intercostals) and the abdomen to function properly in controlling the release of air.

A good initial exercise for breathing awareness is for the singers to take their hands and place them on their sides with their thumbs on the bottoms of their rib cages. In this posture (shown in the photo to the left), have them take several deep breaths. If they are breathing correctly, their thumbs will be pushed out, reflecting the expansion that occurs on the sides and back of the abdominal area.

Placement

The Singing Tone

A proper singing tone may be defined as one where each vowel has a resonant, ringing sound. Singers who have properly developed this tone will have a feeling of buzz or zing in the masque of the face, behind the eyes—the area where the singer has the sensation of producing sound. This buzz is the result of sympathetic vibrations in the nasal cavities, resulting from the proper working of the pharynx. Singers may be encouraged to find a ringing tone through the use of mental images to feel the tone "behind the eyes," "higher in the head," or to think of the vocal tone as "being forward."

Singers must patiently work to find a ringing sound for each vowel, throughout their range: every vowel, on any pitch, should have resonance that sounds and feels aligned in the same area of the singer's face. With the vowels aligned correctly, the singer has a sensation of projecting the vocal tone off the hard palate (the roof of your mouth). It is quite common, for example, for young singers to allow open vowels like "ah" and "oh" to fall back in their throats, while vowels like "ee" or "ay" will be brighter but shallow. Trained singers avoid these pitfalls, consistently singing reverberant vowels. A relaxed throat, an energetic breath, a high soft palate, and a bright forward feeling will greatly aid in producing well-aligned vowels.

Part of the issue with tone production, and why it is a sensitive subject, is that singing involves internal muscles and cartilage in the larynx and throat which we are unable to control manually. We do control the vocal mechanism in various other ways: by lifting the soft palate, and manipulating the lip, jaw, and mouth in myriad ways, in addition to supplying the vocal mechanism with a steady, easy current of air.

Today, more and more choral conductors are well-versed in matters of vocal pedagogy. If they are not accomplished singers in their own right (a great many are), then they have probably read widely and thought about the issues involved. College and university course work for budding conductors should include intensive vocal study. Many convention sessions and professional journal articles have been and continue to be dedicated to the topics of vocal health, the changing voice, the young singer, and so forth. In short, there is little excuse for choral directors not to have a thorough, working knowledge of the singing voice.

A properly produced voice will be free of unwanted muscular tension in the neck, shoulders, and upper body. It will enjoy a warm, bright resonance, and will have an easy, flexible vibrato. Voices that are not properly produced may lack warmth, may often be out of tune, or may have an edge or harshness to the sound.

Choral Tone

The issue of choral tone is a thorny one; it is the subject of much debate and little agreement, not only today but from long ago in the past. Some conductors prefer a straight tone, without much vibrato at all. Others spend much time matching vowels and pronunciations among singers.

A healthy choral tone is built on a low, energized breath.

My own preferences for choral tone are based on my experience singing for one of my former teachers, the late Robert Fountain. He encouraged a free, easy choral sound built on a low, active center of breath in the body, combined with open, relaxed vowel sounds. Each spring, we sang a difficult two-hour program for eight or ten nights on tour. Each day included long bus rides, rehearsals before the concert, and then the concert itself. The proof, for me, that his was a sensible approach to choral singing lay in the fact that at the end of these tours, our voices were in fine shape. It is an approach to the issue of choral tone and healthy choral singing that I strongly advocate.

Synthesis

A correctly produced vocal sound begins with proper posture, frequently reinforced in rehearsal. It is essential for the choral director to constantly remind singers about matters of posture, when both sitting and standing. Secondly, the sound must be energized by a full, active breath centered low in the body, supporting a ringing tone on each vowel throughout the singers' ranges. Conductors must vigilantly watch for and listen for signs of good vocal health. Perhaps only in the case of an ensemble of professional singers will the choral director be exempt from repeatedly working on basic vocal principles.

Differences between solo and choral singing

Some might argue that there are vast differences between the techniques used for solo singing versus those for singing in a choir. I think today that this is not so, although it may have been at one point in time. There are, however, two points that bear momentary consideration.

Choral singers usually need to breathe together, normally one beat before the first note of singing. This often leads to a fast, quick breath. Solo singers are often encouraged to breathe more slowly, over a longer period of time (a luxury the soloist may afford to him or herself). This difference in approach is not critical, but a conductor should encourage her choir to breathe more slowly and deeply when the musical situation allows it. And conductors should guard against the taking of shallow, gasping breaths in their ensembles that quick breathing can sometimes lead to.

Vowel production in a choir is directly related to that most important of musical concerns, timbre. This is no different than with a solo singer. Conductors spend quite a large amount of time trying to make vowel sounds that are similar throughout a section and across the choir. Note that I have not said "the same" vowel sound. It is nearly impossible for two different singers (with different physiognomies) to produce exactly the same vowel sound, especially across the vowel spectrum. But singers can be asked to listen to each other and produce similar sounds. And it is possible to do this without interfering with a singer's private study or to interfere with what works best for him and his voice. The "oh" vowel can be produced with so many subtle variances, even for a soloist, that asking one singer to listen to another and for the two of them to approach a similar sound is merely a way to color a vowel through its shape.

Experienced conductors will learn that ensembles have their own innate timbre. My Concert Choir in one year does not always sound like the choir of the previous year. If I have had little turnover in the choir, for example, the sound may be more robust or richer because the relative age of the students is slightly older. Every choir of forty-five singers sounds like themselves, not like any other choir of forty-five: the sound is unique to that specific set of human beings. And of course, we try to sing Baroque music differently than we sing Brahms (with different articulations and a different weight in the sound), which also only adds to the timbral mix available to the choir as an ensemble.

Vocal Warm-Ups

Vocal warm-ups serve many purposes. Among these are:

- To focus the attention of the singer on the rehearsal or performance about to take place
- To physically warm-up the vocal mechanism, much like stretching before vigorous exercise

- To focus the ear on intonation and listening skills
- To teach vocal concepts or techniques that you will use either in the immediate rehearsal, or over the long term

The choral director may attack any number of vocal or musical problems through vocalizations and warm-ups, including proper breathing, placement, tuning, vowel production, consonant articulation, music reading, etc.

There are two kinds of vocalizations and warm-ups. In the first category are those that deal with physically warming up the vocal instrument and reinforcing correct vocal technique. Begin with exercises that enliven the breathing process and relax the face/neck muscles. These may include physical exercises such as stretching, posture-enhancing strategies, hissing, neck and shoulder rubs, etc. Include at least one exercise that focuses on placing the breath low in the body, in a physically active manner. For example:

I like to use one of these to begin most rehearsals to encourage an active, low center of breath support in the body, transposing up by a half-step the exercise (and all subsequent warm-ups at each repetition).

Next, I incorporate vocalises that focus on sound placement, using primarily open vowels. Keep the range of these initial vocalizes short (within a third or a fifth). Then move to vocalises that increase in pitch range. Usually, these ascend in pitch so the higher voices (sopranos and tenors) can learn to use their upper voices; however, sometimes they should go lower so that basses and altos can learn to sing properly in their bottom tessituras. I use the two exercises that follow to encourage legato singing and an open, relaxed vocal production

Or I will use an exercise that combines both an active breath with an expanded range:

Finally, there should be a harmonic exercise, where the ensemble must sing chords together, listening intently for intonation, matching vowel sounds and vowel alignment, and achieving a good balance between voice parts. Here is one example:

The second category of vocalization pertains to correcting specific technical or musical problems you expect to encounter in the rehearsal, or that you may have encountered previously. This may include isolating from the score melodies or rhythms that are difficult. It might also include a passage of music taken from the literature you are about to rehearse.

Alternating types of warm-up patterns (ascending vs. descending, fast vs. slow, etc.) produces the best results. Exercises should also include more than one vowel sound: not only do singers need to correctly phonate individual vowels, they should also do so in combinations, since they will have to do exactly that when singing real texts. Mix open vowels (ah, oh, oo) with those that are closed (ay, ee, ai). The choral director should consider ending the warm-up period with a vocalization that makes the most direct connection to the first piece of music to be rehearsed. For instance, if the initial piece is one that involves long, legato vocal lines, finish your vocalizing with an exercise demanding long, sustained vocalism. Many choral directors have found success excerpting a particular passage from the repertoire being studied and transforming it into a vocalise. Although choral directors may differ about the actual vocalises that might work best in a particular situation, there should be no argument about one matter: warming up the voice is an absolute necessity at every rehearsal.

Vocal warm-ups are essential at every rehearsal, and before every performance.

There are literally thousands of effective vocalises. You should develop a set of these that works well with your choir, one that addresses their specific vocal needs. Vocalises can be accompanied by the piano (it is best to progress either up or down by half steps), or the vocalises may be performed unaccompanied (which is beneficial for the students' ear-training).

There are advantages to using the same or similar vocal exercises at each rehearsal. By doing so, singers are free to concentrate on the vocal mechanism and correct singing rather than having to learn new exercises frequently. The downside is obvious, of course: singers may simply get used to the drill and sing on autopilot, without carefully focusing on what they are doing.

Several other vocalises that I use frequently follow. The two just below combine a forward, bright focus (emphasizing the "ng" of "ming") before opening to the vowel sound.

To allow the altos and basses to explore the lower portion of their ranges, and to teach them to sing without pushing and to keep the sound focused forward, I often use this exercise, moving downwards by half-steps in pitch:

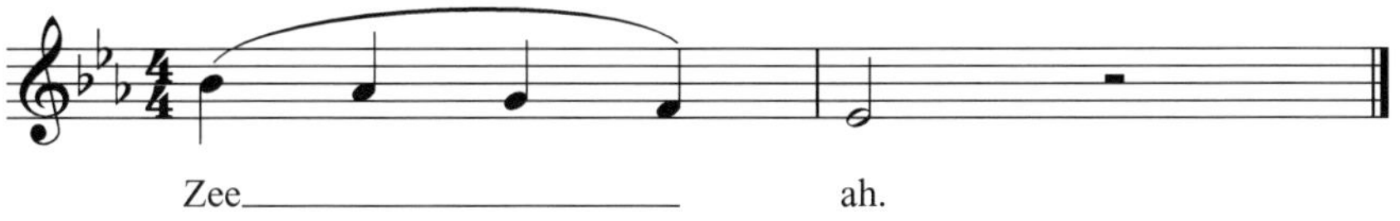

The two exercises that follow explore a wider range. The second of these allows for a similar pattern in all the voices, without making the lower voices strain to reach higher notes, or higher voices push too low in their ranges.

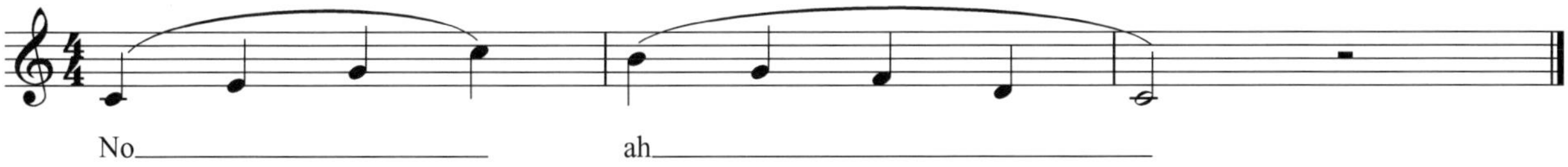

Vocal Ranges

Although there are differences of opinion among choral conductors and voice teachers, the following vocal ranges might be taken as a guideline.

High School Voices

Mature Voices

There is often confusion about vocal terminology. What is a second alto? Mezzo-soprano? Bass vs. baritone? Coloratura soprano? In general, choral composers specify the vocal parts as shown above, although it is common to find split parts, such as Soprano I and II or Bass I and II. Terms such as mezzo-soprano and dramatic baritone more often apply to certain types of solo voices, as determined by range, quality, and the kinds of roles available to them in opera, oratorio, and musical theatre. Singers, even in high school, should be classified not only by their ranges but by the quality of the sound they produce. Pay careful attention to how young singers produce pitches at the top and bottom of their voice ranges. Straining to hit high notes, or compressing the larynx to squeeze out low notes, are good indications that the singer is pushing towards limits that are uncomfortable. Categorize their voices accordingly.

Evaluating Voices

It is imperative that every voice in a choir be evaluated every year at least once at the beginning of the season. Especially with young singers, you may also find it helpful to test some voices periodically throughout the year. It is especially important to conduct vigilant voice testing on a regular basis when your students are not actively studying voice in the private studio, as they don't have the individual guidance a voice teacher provides.

The purpose of the initial voice test is two-fold: to determine the range and quality of each individual singer; and to make sure that each singer is singing with a healthy, well-produced voice. The purposes of the follow-up evaluations throughout the year are the same, and with the added responsibility to make adjustments for the singers if their voices have changed in any way. It is also a good idea to tell your singers to keep you informed if their assigned vocal part seems too low or high so you can adjust their part assignment accordingly.

The voice test may be kept simple, including the choice of easy, quickly assimilated vocalises. Try to hear the voice on an ascending and a descending exercise (for they will show different capabilities of the voice), and watch for physical signs, particularly with younger singers, that you are extending them either too high or too low. Two telltale signs, both pictured below, are a protruding jaw (on left) or a compressed larynx (on right).

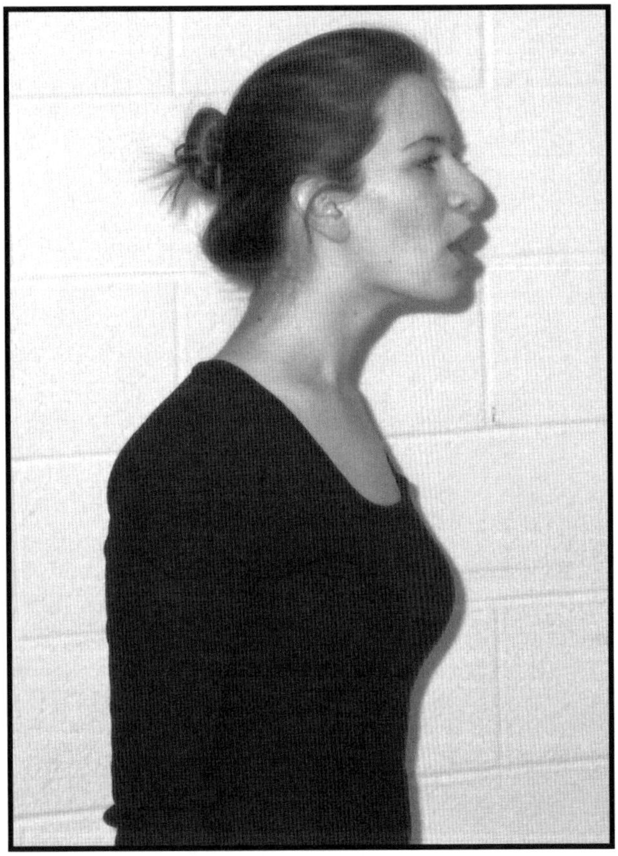
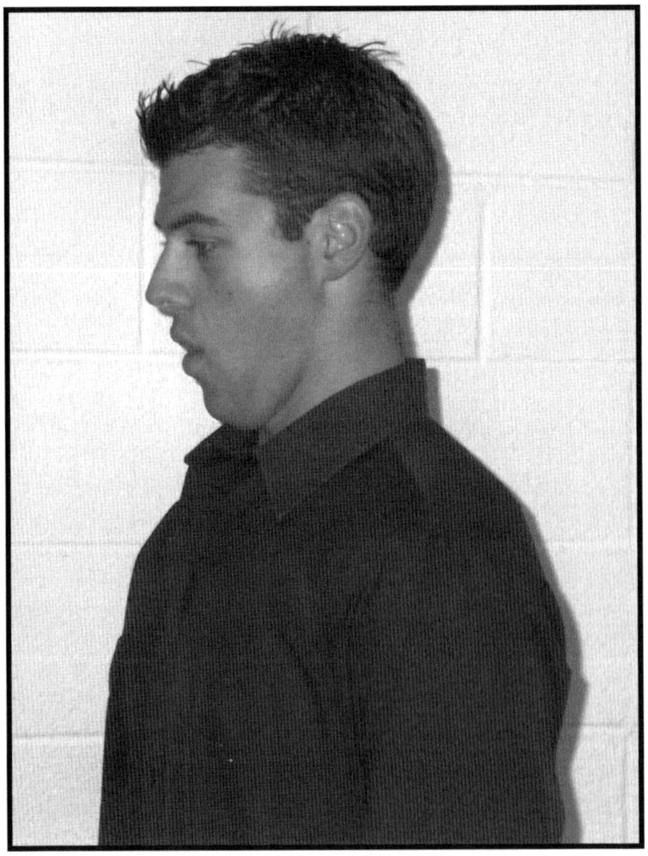

Seating the Choir

One of the most important tasks for the choral conductor is the seating of the choir. In some ways, the instrumental conductor may have a slight advantage in this regard because of the limitations imposed on the seating possibilities by the numbers of instruments represented, and by historical convention. While some of these same kinds of issues are present for the choral conductor, there are many more seating alternatives for a choir, and hence, increased complexity.

There are several broad considerations in seating the choir:

- The individual singer's vocal quality and musical ability
- The placement of individual singers next to each other within each voice section
- The numbers of singers on each voice part, and the relative ability level of each section
- The repertoire being rehearsed
- The shape and size of the rehearsal space and the performance venue

A large number of studies have been conducted (and theses written) about choral seating arrangements, differing widely in their conclusions. Some conductors spend a great deal of time seating every student according to voice type. Among the considerations are the differences between strong voices and lighter ones; voices with a bright timbre and those with darker tones; heavy voices versus those with comparatively little vibrato; and so forth. Conductors must also take into account music-reading skills, confidence as a singer, etc. Here are several generalizations that might be helpful:

- Seat weaker sight-readers next to better readers.
- Don't sit two darker, heavier voices next to each other. Place these voices throughout the section.
- Try to keep the heavier voices out of the front row.
- Put more confident singers, including those with the better aural skills, on the ends of the rows and in the back of the choir, where their skills may be needed.

Of course, there is also the one thing that tends to get in the way of the best-laid seating plans: taller singers usually need to go in the upper rows (and shorter singers in the front rows), sometimes in defiance of the other guidelines!

The two seating arrangements shown below are fairly standard when there are nearly equal numbers of voices in each principal section.

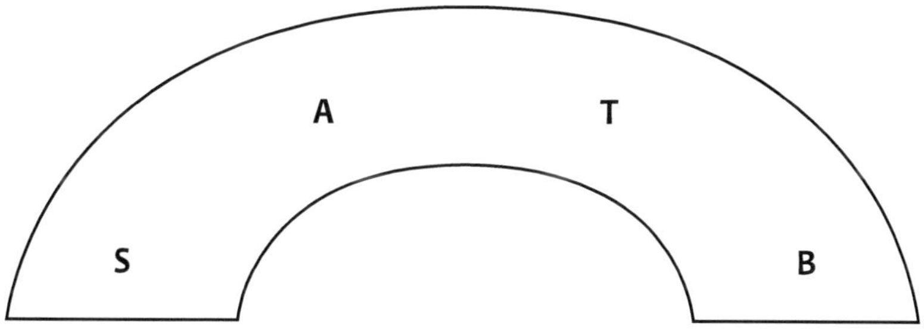

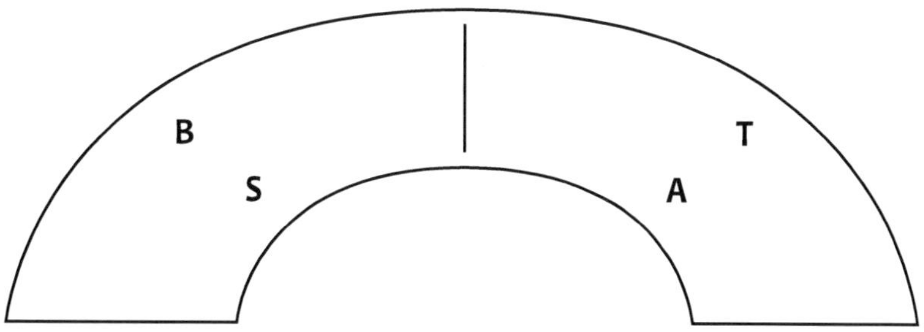

In the first example, the arrangement is obvious: the choir is seated in "score order" (highest to lowest) across the choir. In the second example, the men are seated behind the women, with the highest and lowest notes (soprano and bass) in close conjunction, and with the middle parts also next to each other (tenors behind the altos). Either of these seating arrangements is very useful for performing music that is largely homophonic, where the parts move together and the ranges rarely cross. In most music of this type (think Mozart, Haydn, or Handel), the melody line and the supportive bass line are most important, with the middle voices filling in the harmonies.

If your choir has one voice part that is significantly fewer in number than the others, it is best to place them forward and center so they project and balance the other voices in the most optimal fashion. In the illustration just below, the tenors (often lacking in numbers) are placed in the front, surrounded by the other voices. This allows their part to better balance the other voices.

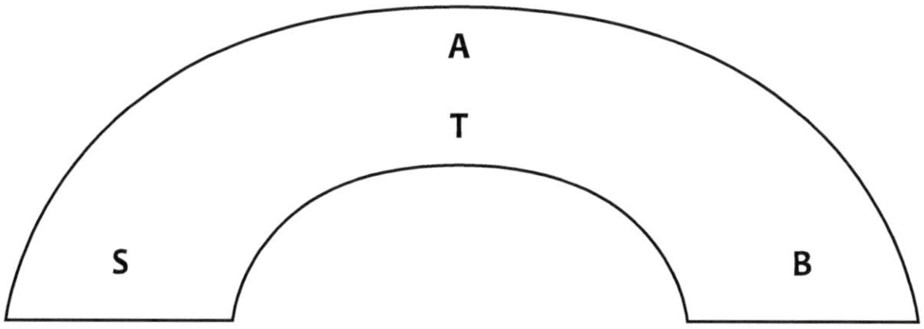

It is also possible to mix the sections by seating everyone in quartets (or double quartets), which will help the singers hear each other wonderfully. But the conductor must be assured that the choristers are very secure on their parts before this kind of arrangement is implemented. Mixed seating arrangements are useful when performing music in which the individual parts are equal, such as music in the Renaissance. I often use this with Romantic and contemporary choral music as well.

There is a great deal of choral literature written for double chorus. I typically seat the two choirs as illustrated below, seating the men behind the women, and keeping the sopranos and basses of each choir together in the middle:

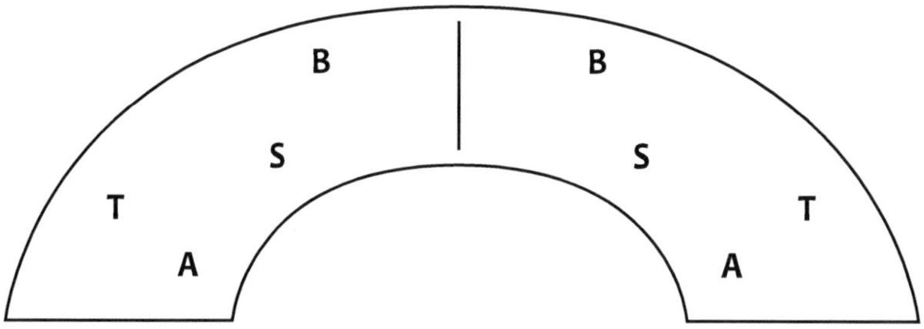

Single-gender choirs—men's and women's choruses—present their own seating challenges. Here are common seating plans for single gender choirs:

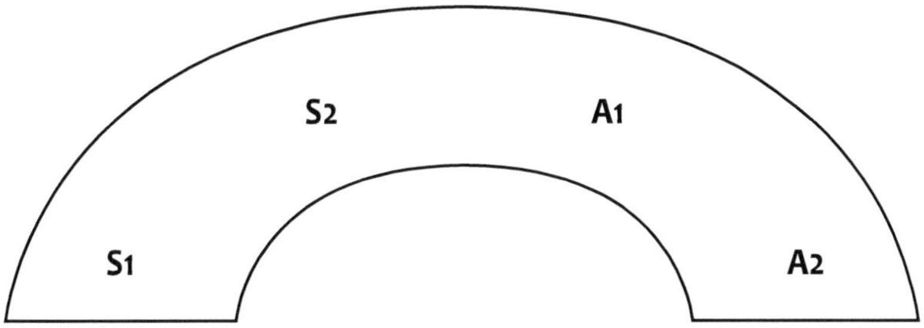

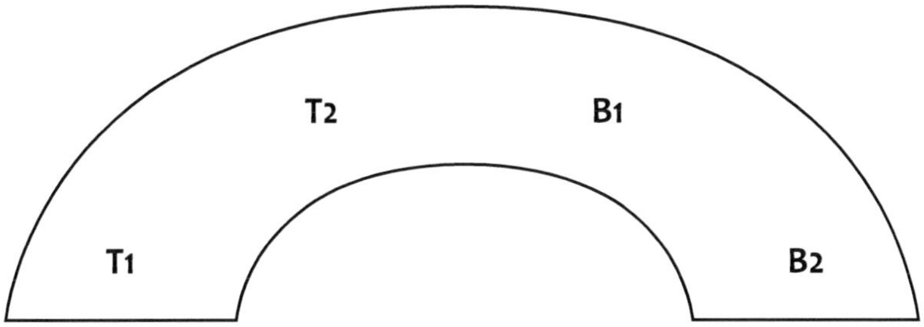

Some conductors will seat their women's choruses in mirror image of the top figure above, with the sopranos on the left side of the choir and the altos on the right. In my men's chorus, I often find I have fewer tenors than baritones and basses. In that case, I use a modification of the SATB arrangement in which the tenors are grouped in the middle of the choir for better balance, placing the baritones to the left side and leaving the basses on the right.

The rules for seating are not set in stone, so conductors should remain flexible—don't be afraid to experiment with different arrangements. I frequently change the standing arrangement of my choir several times during a concert, having them sing some numbers in a sectional formation and then switching to a mixed standing arrangement (usually in mixed quartets) for other pieces. We switch again if we sing something calling for a double choir-formation. Regardless of what arrangement you choose, make sure your choir settles into a particular seating/standing formation well before a scheduled concert. Anticipate in advance what will happen when the singers step on to the choral risers, and then rehearse in that formation regularly before the concert. If feasible, rehearse in the actual performance space several times.

Getting Better: Observing Other Conductors

One of the best ways to learn to conduct is by closely observing more experienced conductors, both in rehearsal and in performance. One may garner many ideas through close study of master conductors in real-life situations. Towards that end, here are some questions that you might ask yourself:

Rehearsal Observation Questions

- What warm-ups are used by the conductor? How do they contribute to vocal health, blend, balance, or to other musical needs?
- Notice the general rehearsal demeanor. How does the conductor communicate with the ensemble (talking, conducting, talking over the singers, eye contact, etc.)? Which man-

ner is most effective, and which seems not to elicit much musical response or change from the choir?

- Observe the conductor's technical apparatus. How does he or she cue? Notice both left- and right-hand gestures, as well as the use of eye contact. How does the conductor get across to the choir musical information of a technical nature (cut-offs, entrances, dynamics, and so forth)?
- How does the conductor assert him or herself in the rehearsal? In other words, what keeps the ensemble on task and moving forward? Is it conducting gesture only, or talking only?
- How often does the conductor stop? How long does he or she talk when stopped? How much time elapses before resuming singing, and is the amount of time appropriate, too quick, or too long? Why do you think so?
- How does the conductor deal with various problems such as wrong notes, bad rhythms, faulty ensemble or changes of dynamics, etc. Does she or he only talk about these problems, or are corrections or correct information shown in the conducting gesture?
- Finally, notice the rehearsal pace. Does the conductor move at an appropriate speed? Does she or he deal with musical problems quickly and effectively? How much does the choir get to sing before they are cut-off for more comments? Does this seem appropriate given the ability level of the choir and the difficulty of the music?

Performance Observation Questions

- How is the clarity of the conducting pattern (or lack of it) reflected in the ensemble's performance? In other words, are entrances and cut-offs clean and together? How does the conductor's gesture ensure this, or impede it?
- How does the conducting pattern reflect the character of the music? In other words, is the pattern straightforward, or does the conductor show things like phrase stresses, etc.? Make note of particular gestures that seem particularly helpful or useful.
- Does the conductor have any gestures that seem to impede good musical line? If so, how do they specifically get in the way?
- How and when does the conductor cue? Does he or she cue everything, or just important entrances? Observe how the hands, eyes, and body language are used by this conductor to help with cues and good ensemble singing.
- How does the conducting style reflect the music in other ways? Does the pattern vary appropriately with the music? Does the conductor show metric stress and phrasing, or just beat patterns? How does he or she deal with dynamics, articulation, or the character of the music?
- Does the conductor seem at home with the score, as if he or she is thinking ahead and anticipating problems?
- In observing the performance and its musical effect, how does the conductor deal with issues of balance, intonation, articulation, dynamics, etc. as the performance is underway?

For Further Study

The topics covered in this chapter are widely covered in the prevailing literature on conducting and rehearsing, in part because conductors seem not to agree on solutions. In fact, experience and careful thought should lead you to your own conclusions about how to work with voices, how to seat them, how to classify them, and so forth.

A number of readings may help you in your search for answers. The late Howard Swan, often called the Dean of American choral conductors, wrote a fine essay, "The Development of a Choral Instrument" (Chapter 1), in *Choral Conducting: A Symposium* (Decker and Herford, cited in the previous chapter). Swan describes historical schools of choral sound in the United States, drawing helpful conclusions for the modern conductor. "Vocal Technique," Chapter 1 of Charles W. Heffernan's *Choral Music: Technique and Artistry* (Prentice Hall, 1982) is also very useful. Wilhelm Ehmann and Frauke Haasemann wrote *Voice Building for Choirs* (Hinshaw Music, 1981) based upon their long collaboration. The book deals specifically with choral warm-ups, their use in the rehearsal, and ways of promoting good vocal habits in young singers. *The Choral Experience: Literature, Materials, and Methods* by Ray Robinson and Allen Winhold (Waveland Press, 1976) contains useful chapters on "The Individual Singer and the Choral Experience" (Chapter 3), "Choral Sound" (Chapter 4), and "Choral Diction" (Chapter 5). Two fine sources by Weston Noble are *Building Beautiful Voices* (Roger Dean Publishing Company, 1995) and *Achieving Choral Blend Through Standing Position* (GIA Publications, 2005).

These same topics, from the choral singer's viewpoint rather than the conductor's, are covered in Chapter 3, "Vocal Technique," in the recent book *The Choral Singer's Survival Guide* by Tony Thornton (Vocal Planet Publishing, 2005).

Recapitulation

In the Renaissance, Baroque, and Classical eras, the task of leading an ensemble in performance commonly fell upon the shoulders of the composer, who was most often present for the performance. Indeed, composers were largely responsible for not only leading the performance, but for writing the piece, creating performance parts, recruiting and training the performers, and arranging the logistics of the concert. When conductors first came into widespread employment, their first task was largely to keep the ensemble together. Gradually during the nineteenth century, the conductor was increasingly called upon to lead works that were written by others. Accordingly, the tasks that conductors undertook became more numerous and some of the duties that previously belonged to the composer were ceded to him.

Today, the conductor fulfills many functions. While these responsibilities were presented in some detail in the preceding chapters, it is useful to set them out here in summary:

- Your primary job as a conductor—the very reason that the position was created—is to maintain an accurate tempo for the ensemble to follow. If you cannot undertake that task satisfactorily, then nothing else you do will much matter. Paradoxically, you are also in charge of subtly varying the tempo when the musical fabric demands it, in such a way that the fabric is organically stretched and linked to musical meaning.

- When the conductor became the person in charge of bringing to the performance an interpretation of the score, he or she in effect became the composer's representative. This necessitates a performance based on dedicated study of the score, its historical genesis, the circumstances surrounding its earlier performances, and the musical language that it employs towards depicting the ideas and emotions that lay underneath and behind the notation on the page.

- The conductor today is charge of programming the concert, choosing not only the music but placing it in order in a meaningful way. This task cannot be fulfilled without a thorough and comprehensive knowledge of choral literature. It further entails careful thought as to how the music of a concert best fits together, and takes into consideration the choir's abilities (vocal, musical, and intellectual), their need for musical growth and development, and the audience's desire for a moving, uplifting, or entertaining experience.

- The conductor is in charge of planning rehearsals in such a manner that the choir learns the music in a logical sequence. The rehearsal process should not only focus on notes and rhythms, but also on the musical context of the work, its style, and finally its meaning.

- The conductor must audition his or her singers, and periodically evaluate their progress. This relies heavily on a thorough knowledge of the vocal mechanism and its workings, and a keen ear and sharp eye for exactly how singers, especially young ones, are producing sound.

- Concert logistics also fall to the conductor to plan: getting the stage set up, seating the choir, planning for participation by accompanists or instrumentalists, printing programs, publicity and marketing, and other such tasks. Increasingly, even for school and church music programs, this entails fund-raising, as well.

To be successful as a conductor is difficult work and it takes years of dedicated study and practice to become an artist. But conducting is a rewarding profession, and you will find, as countless choral conductors before you have, that the opportunity to make music with other human beings, their voices raised in song together, is an experience that is truly transcending. The choir is the King of Instruments, and those lucky enough to partake in the conducting of a choir as their chosen profession are well and truly blessed.

About the Author

David P. DeVenney has established a wide reputation as a conductor and scholar. His choirs have toured throughout the United States, Canada, and Europe, receiving acclaim for their carefully prepared and musically exciting performances from audiences and critics alike. His conducting repertory includes over one hundred major choral works with orchestra and two dozen operas and musicals, and he has commissioned and premiered numerous new choral works by noteworthy composers such as David Conte, Robert Maggio, Jennifer Higdon, Emma Lou Diemer, Marvin Hamlisch, and Robert Page. His choirs appear commercially on the Albany label as well as on several private CDs with his university ensembles, and have appeared at state and regional conferences of the Ohio Choral Directors Association and the College Music Society. He regularly collaborates with professional ensembles, conducting the Reading Symphony Orchestra, the Philadelphia Classical Symphony, the Brandywine Ballet, and several others. He received the 2003 Dean's Award for Artistic Excellence from West Chester University and the 2006 Distinguished Music Alumnus award from Iowa State University, and has several times been named Outstanding Teacher by the WCU Honors College.

Dr. DeVenney holds degrees in conducting from Iowa State University, the University of Wisconsin-Madison, and the University of Cincinnati College–Conservatory of Music. He is professor of music at West Chester University, where he directs the select Concert Choir and the Men's Chorus and guides the graduate program in choral studies. For over a decade, he was music director of the Reading Choral Society, a highly regarded community chorus and one of America's oldest musical ensembles. He founded and for seven seasons served as music director of VocalBaroque, a professional chamber choir in Columbus, Ohio. He has held faculty appointments at Otterbein College, the University of Arizona, and Virginia Tech.

Dr. DeVenney has made substantive contributions to scholarship in American choral music through his fourteen books and nearly six dozen articles. *The Choral Journal* called him "one of the most industrious scholars on the current scene," while *MLA Notes* labeled his contributions to the study of American choral music "an impressive achievement."

Also by David P. DeVenney

Reference

Nineteenth-century American Choral Music: An Annotated Guide

Early American Choral Music: An Annotated Guide

American Masses and Requiems: A Descriptive Guide

American Choral Music Since 1920: An Annotated Guide

The Chorus in Opera: A Guide to the Repertory (with Craig R. Johnson)

The Broadway Song Companion

The New Broadway Song Companion (revised edition)

History and Cultural Studies

Source Readings in American Choral Music

Varied Carols: A Survey of American Choral Literature

Forging America: New Lands and High Culture